Laws
&
Writs of Appeal

1647–1663

New Netherland Documents Series
Volume XVI, part one

Engraving of Hugo Grotius
Courtesy of the Royal Library at The Hague

Laws
&
Writs of Appeal
1647–1663

Translated and Edited by
CHARLES T. GEHRING

SYRACUSE UNIVERSITY PRESS

The paper used in this publication meets the minimum requirements of American National Standard for Information Sciences—Permanence of Paper for Printed Library Materials, ANSI Z 39.48–1984. ∞™

Produced with the support of The Holland Society of New York and the New Netherland Project of the New York State Library

The preparation of this volume was made possible in part by a grant from the Division of Research Programs of the National Endowment for the Humanities, an independent federal agency.

This book is published with the assistance of a grant from the John Ben Snow Foundation.

Library of Congress Cataloging-in-Publication Data

New Netherland.
    Laws & writs of appeal, 1647–1663 / translated and edited by
Charles T. Gehring.
        p.   cm.   —   (New Netherland documents)
    "XVI, part one."
    Includes bibliographical references and index.
    ISBN 0-8156-2522-7
    1. Law—New York (State) 2. Law reports, digests, etc.—New York
(State)   I. Gehring, Charles T., 1939–   . II. Title. III. Title:
Laws and writs of appeal, 1647–1663.   IV. Series.
KFN5030.5.G44   1991
348.747'028—dc20
[347.470828]   91-13990
                                                                  CIP

MANUFACTURED IN THE UNITED STATES OF AMERICA

This volume is dedicated to the

Netherland–America Foundation

in gratitude for its promotion
of cultural relations between
our two countries, and
its support of historical programs
devoted to the Dutch experience
in the New World.

Charles T. Gehring was born in Fort Plain, an old Erie Canal town in New York State's Mohawk Valley. After completing his undergraduate and graduate studies at Virginia Military Institute and West Virginia University he continued with post graduate work at Albert–Ludwigs–Universität in Freiburg, Germany. There he began his study of the Dutch language and first realized that his future research lay much closer to home. He eventually received a Ph.D. in Germanic Linguistics from Indiana University with a concentration in Netherlandic Studies. His dissertation (1973) was a linguistic investigation of the survival of the Dutch language in colonial New York. He is presently director of the New Netherland Project (sponsored by the New York State Library), which is responsible for translating the official records of the Dutch colony and promoting awareness of the Dutch role in American history. He has been a fellow of the Holland Society of New York since 1979.

Committee on Publication

Contents

Acknowledgments

I wish to express my gratitude to the staff of the New Netherland Project: Martha Dickinson Shattuck, Jansje Venema, and Nancy Anne McClure Zeller, who were involved in every stage of production from transcribing to editing; to Florence and Peter Christoph who stepped in at the last minute and produced the index.

Finally, I wish to thank Jerome Yavarkovsky, director of the New York State Library, for his expert advice to the New Netherland Project; to the Holland Society of New York for its steadfast support of the translation and publication of records relating to our Dutch heritage; to the staff of the New York State Library for its highly professional assistance; to all the contributors to the New Netherland Project; to the Friends of the New Netherland Project; to the Division of Research Programs of the National Endowment for the Humanities whose financial support through a matching grant made the translation possible; and to the Netherland–America Foundation, whose financial assistance provided a considerable amount of the funds necessary to match the NEH grant.

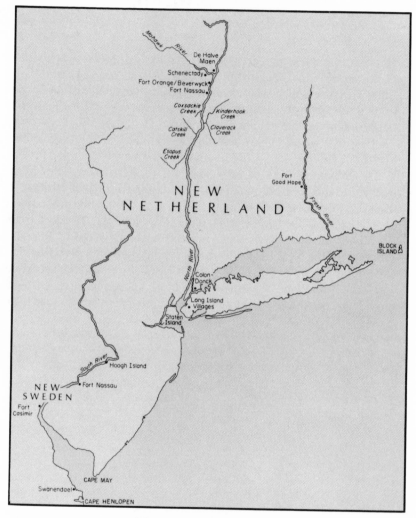

Map of New Netherland
Courtesy of the Albany Institute of History & Art

Introduction

The Dutch West India Company

By 1609 the Hapsburg Empire had tacitly recognized the existence of the United Provinces of the Netherlands. After more than forty years of unsuccessful attempts to stamp out this revolt in the low countries, Spain sought a period of time to lick its wounds and consolidate its hold on the ten lower provinces. The Twelve Years' Truce was mostly the work of Johan van Oldenbarnevelt, pensionary of Holland, who represented the agenda of the remonstrants: religious toleration, decentralized government, and peace with Spain. This party was identified with the followers of Arminius, a theologian at the University of Leiden, who called for a less rigid interpretation of the Reformed Church's doctrine of predestination. Arminius was strongly opposed by a fellow theologian at Leiden named Gomarus, an adherent of a strict interpretation of predestination. He led the counter-remonstrants in their drive for a national religion under the Reformed Church, a strong centralized government, and renewal of the war with Spain.

What should have been twelve years of peace turned out to be more than a decade of turmoil and near civil war. When Maurits, the prince of Orange, son of Willem the Silent, saw the advantage of supporting the Gomarists and consolidating his power by becoming the leader of a strong centralized government once again at war with his archenemy, he convened the Synod of Dordrecht in order to resolve the theological debate. With Prince Maurits's support the Gomarist position won the day. Van Oldenbarnevelt was arrested, tried, and beheaded on trumped up charges of treason. Hugo Grotius, the great legal mind of the Netherlands and strong advocate of the Arminian position, was also arrested and sentenced to life in prison. After three years under confinement, Grotius's wife managed to smuggle him out in a crate used to transport his research books in and out of prison. He spent the rest of his years in exile in France and Sweden. While in prison, however, he did make good use of the books that his wife brought him by writing the famous *Inleiding tot de Hollandsche Rechtsgeleerdheid,* or "Introduction to the Jurisprudence of Holland." With the death of Van Oldenbarnevelt and the exile of Grotius the Netherlands had lost its greatest and most eloquent advocates of peace. In 1621 the truce was allowed to lapse and war with Spain was resumed.

The East India Company had been in operation as a joint-stock trading venture since 1602. Chartered by the States General of the Netherlands, the East India Company had a trading monopoly from the Cape of Good Hope east to the Strait of Magellan. It had the power to raise its own armies and navies, make alliances with local sovereigns within its sphere of operations, and if necessary could make war and conclude peace in defense of its interests. Company shares were traded on the Amsterdam stock exchange and investors represented a broad spectrum of society: from wealthy merchants to tavern keepers and bar maids. At the conclusion of the Twelve Years' Truce, the States General saw an opportunity to privatize the overseas war with Spain by chartering another joint-stock venture with a trading monopoly from the Cape of Good Hope westward to the outer reaches of New Guinea. The company was divided into five chambers at Amsterdam, Zeeland (Middelburgh), Maes (Rotterdam), *Noorderquartier* (Hoorn and Enkhuizen), and Groningen-Friesland. The number of directors on the governing board was determined by the chambers' financial obligation. As the largest investor Amsterdam sent six, followed by Zeeland with four, and the other three chambers with two each; the States General sent one representative for a total of nineteen. This powerful board was known as *de heeren negentien*, i.e., "the lords nineteen," often represented in documents by the roman numerals *XIX*. Thus the West India Company (WIC) was formed more as an instrument of war than a vehicle of commerce. Whereas nineteen years earlier the East India Company was able to raise six and a half million guilders in one month to capitalize its enterprise, it took the WIC two years to raise seven million guilders. As soon as ships were outfitted and equipped, the WIC made its presence felt against enemy colonies and interests from Africa to Brazil. Especially vulnerable were the possessions of Portugal, which had been united under the Spanish crown since 1580. WIC preoccupation with lucrative interests in Africa, Brazil, and the Caribbean, however, left few resources, either human or monetary, for its fur trading outpost in North America.

New Netherland

When Henry Hudson, sailing for the East India Company in 1609, explored Delaware Bay and the river to the north now carrying his name, little did he know that it would be the foundation of a Dutch claim to a massive territory from Cape Henlopen at the mouth of

Delaware Bay to the Connecticut River. From these chance maneuverings between what would become New England and the tobacco colonies of Maryland and Virginia developed a colony that had its roots in Europe rather than in England. For the greater part of the seventeenth century not only would the Netherlands compete with England for the mastery of the high seas, but also obstruct her drive for hegemony in North America.

Shortly after Hudson's explorations various trading companies were licensed by the States General to trade with the natives in the major waterways from Maine to Virginia. By 1614, competition between traders had become so fierce and bloody that the New Netherland Company was chartered as a monopoly to trade in the region in order to stabilize the situation. Trading cartels were allowed to send out four voyages within three years between the latitudes of 40 and 45 degrees (Barnegat Bay, New Jersey, and Eastport, Maine). The main base of operations became Fort Nassau, which was built to serve as a trading post on Castle Island, now mostly occupied by the port of Albany. From this post expeditions were sent into the interior in search of mineral deposits to exploit, and an active trade with the natives was carried on. When the charter expired in 1618 and Fort Nassau was destroyed by a spring freshet, the territory was once again open to cut-throat trading activities. Although the WIC was chartered in 1621 it took almost two years for it to raise enough money to finance its first effort to take possession of its holdings along the Delaware, Hudson, and Connecticut Rivers.

After some initial experiments with satellite trading posts supported by agricultural communities on the three major river systems, Manhattan was chosen as the administrative center of the colony and the place most suitable for warehousing and trans-shipping furs to the Netherlands; the island had an ideal harbor, free of ice year round, and was large enough to establish any number of support farms. In spite of some serious mistakes in the early years with the Mohawks, the easternmost nation of Iroquois, the Dutch forged a strong alliance with this tribe that controlled the most important trade route to the interior. At first the colony grew slowly and almost seemed to stagnate. People wishing to leave the Netherlands chose other places to seek their fortunes: France, England, East India Company colonies, and the WIC's own colony of New Holland in Brazil. New Netherland was still not thought to be particularly inviting. However, every year brought more and more displaced persons into the Netherlands, fleeing the disruptions of the Baltic wars, the Thirty Years' War, and religious persecution in France, not to mention the disruption in the United Provinces caused by the protracted war with

Spain. By the 1650s, however, these displaced persons would also be considering New Netherland for their future home.

Several factors led to an improved climate in the colony. The end of the disastrous Indian wars under director general Kieft were followed by increased trading activity with the English colonies as a result of the turmoil created by the civil war in England. A series of inept administrators had forced the directors in Amsterdam to take more care in the selection process. In 1647 Petrus Stuyvesant arrived as director general, furnishing the colony with a firm and fair hand. The fall of New Holland in Brazil to the Portuguese in 1654 freed up WIC human and financial resources for its long-neglected colony in North America. The end of the first Anglo-Dutch war in 1654 created a feeling of optimism in the colony, and, of course, a false sense of security. Increased activity of private traders, especially encouraged by Stuyvesant's relations with the Caribbean, augured well for the future. Finally, the elimination of New Sweden on the Delaware as a political and commercial competitor led to the city of Amsterdam's establishment of a colony. With its benefactor's wealth and ready immigrants, New Amstel had a bright future. However, all this changed when Charles II, king of England, granted the territory containing New Netherland to his brother James, duke of York and Albany. The Dutch would return in 1673 during the third Anglo-Dutch war and regain the colony as easily as it was lost nine years earlier, only to bargain it away at the treaty of Westminster.

Colonial Administration

The success of a colonial administrator in New Netherland depended as much on luck, intuitive judgment, and the courage to make bold decisions on matters often supported only by faulty intelligence and rumor, as it did on strict adherence to WIC instructions. Directors of the colony often had to wait over a year to receive approval of requests, reaction to decisions, and clarification and amplification of WIC policy. In some cases pressing matters had been disposed of long before instructions or approval were received from Amsterdam. Directors such as Verhulst, Minuit, Van Twiller, and Kieft all proved to be unsuited to the task of operating a remote colony under these conditions. All returned to the Netherlands either under a cloud of mismanagement or ineptitude. Even Stuyvesant provoked the Amsterdam directors with his actions; but his errors always seemed to be the result of boldness and decisiveness rather than pettiness and inertia.

The earliest surviving instructions for directors of the colony are those issued to Willem Verhulst in 1625. They state with utter simplicity the structure of government to be observed. Verhulst was to serve as director of the colony assisted by a council, which consisted of his commissary, secretary, *schout*, and any skippers in port at the time.* This body carried out all executive, legislative and judicial functions of the colony. The instructions also dealt with specific legal matters, such as the punishment for persons who illegally slaughtered animals. However, the director was instructed to observe and obey the ordinances and customs of Holland in matters concerning marriage, settlement of estates, and contracts; and in cases of intestate estates to observe the placard issued by the States of Holland in 1587. There is a reference in the instructions that copies of these papers had been sent. Finally, the director was admonished not to pass any new laws or ordinances or sanction any new customs without the approval of the WIC directors. Even after the colony had grown in population and new communities had sprung up from Beverwijck in the north to Fort Casimir in the south, the nature of this highly centralized governing body remained essentially the same.

In 1644 the first court other than that of the central administration on Manhattan was formed at Heemstede. This court, which was in response to an influx of settlers from Connecticut, was followed by one at Gravesande in 1645 and one at Breuckelen in 1646. The increase of population on Manhattan was accompanied by an increase in legal activity: lawsuits, petty squabbles, and other nuisances best handled by arbitrators rather than the full central council. In order to keep the council from being swamped by such cases, a court of arbitrators, consisting of nine men, was established in 1647. Their function was to decide cases referred to them by the council; however, judgments were subject to appeal before the council. This board relieved the council of its increasingly heavy case load until February of 1653, when New Amsterdam received its charter as a municipality. The court of arbitrators was at this time replaced by a court of *schout*, burgomasters and *schepenen*. Other benches of justice were erected at Flushing in 1648, Beverwijck and Middelburgh in 1652, Amesfoort and Midwout in 1654, Westchester and Rustdorp (Jamaica) in 1656, Haerlem in 1660, Bushwijck, Wiltwijck (Kingston), Bergen, and New Utrecht in 1661, and Staten Island in 1664. The laws and ordinances enacted by the council on Manhattan were binding in all communities within New Netherland, unless they exclusively applied to a specific locality. Attempts by the patroonships, especially Rensselaerswijck, to exercise their independence and remain outside the jurisdiction of the council's ordinances, led to disputes that eventually were resolved in favor of the WIC. By 1658 Rensselaerswijck

---

* Verhulst's instructions can be found in *Documents Relating to New Netherland, 1624–1626*, A. J. F. van Laer, trans. and ed. (San Marino, CA, 1924).

was required to post WIC ordinances in its jurisdiction and submit its own ordinances for approval by the council on Manhattan as did all other communities in New Netherland.

Although the council on Manhattan served as a control on ordinances submitted by inferior courts, it too had to submit its ordinances to the scrutiny of the directors in Amsterdam. Several times ordinances were returned with the directors' expression of disapproval. Once the council was sternly advised to adhere strictly to the customs and ordinances of the city of Amsterdam, a copy of which had been supplied the council for consultation, in order to prevent such future conflicts. Another time certain resolutions adopted by the *lantdach*, an assembly consisting of representatives from the inferior courts, were rejected by the directors, who found it especially strange that the resolutions had been published without waiting for their approval. When ordinances were approved by the directors, they were sometimes revised and then returned to New Netherland in printed form. Unfortunately, none of these printed copies of ordinances is still among the records.

The laws of Holland, according to which the council on Manhattan was to regulate itself, had been systematized by Hugo Grotius in his *Introduction to the Jurisprudence of Holland*, which had appeared in 1631. By this work Grotius contributed to making Roman–Dutch law accessible as a legal system. As with the legal systems of other countries, Holland's system of law reflected the various stages of its historical development and the effect of outside influences. From the ancient customs derived from Germanic law, to the considerable influence of the Roman code of Justinian (the *corpus juris*), to the canon law of the Catholic Church, to the special privileges gained from support of one monarch or another, they had all contributed to the confused mass of law that Grotius was able to systematize in such a clear and concise manner. It soon became regarded as the authoritative work on Roman-Dutch law and rose rapidly in popularity because it was written in Dutch rather than Latin.

In addition to Grotius, the council on Manhattan, and probably the inferior courts, including those of the patroonships, would have had copies of the following works at their disposal: *Ordonantie van de Policien binnen Hollandt*, usually cited simply as the "Political Ordinance." Published shortly after the Union of Utrecht in 1580, it was the States of Holland's response to the massive confusion in the laws of the province. This early attempt to bring some uniformity to legal matters regarding marriage, succession, sales, leases, mortgages and registration would have been a standard reference for the courts of New Netherland. Other works included Joost van Damhouder's *Praktycq Crimineel*, one of the earliest treatments of criminal procedure, and Paul Merula's 1592 treatise on the *Civil Procedure of the Courts of Holland, Zeeland and West Friesland*, which was considered the standard work on the practice of the Dutch superior courts. The directors also sent over a copy of the *Groot Placaetboek van Amsterdam*, which was a compilation of the edicts and ordinances of the city of Amsterdam. Not only were these legal volumes available in the colony, but also the uniformity and precision of the legal proceedings indicate that they were actively consulted.

The Dutch Colonial Manuscripts

In 1689, shortly after Jacob Leisler assumed control of the New York provincial government, an inventory was made of the records in the office of the provincial secretary. Following the various English records appears an entry which simply indicates the presence of "some old Dutch record books and bundles of papers." Not until 1821 do we find out more details about these Dutch records. In that year Secretary of State Christopher Yates ordered another inventory of the records in his office, in which each Dutch record book was listed with a short description of its contents. Among the forty-some books carrying the original Dutch alphabetical designations are: "No. 13 Book marked M contains laws and regulations from 1647 to 1658"; and "No. 14 Book marked N contains the Burgomasters' laws and ordinances of 1656." These books are the source of the records in the first part of this volume. The writs of appeal contained in the second part are not recorded as a separate entity in the inventory. They may have been recorded in another record book, or they may have been unbound and among the bundles of papers mentioned in 1689.

Ideally these record books should have been preserved in their original state. Not only is it important for the historian to know that the juxtaposition of records was the result of the secretary or clerk operating under the pressures and exigencies of the period, but that certain idiosyncrasies and anomalies reveal certain details about the operations of various officials and administrations otherwise lost. For example, it was the style of one secretary to record all the ordinances for a given year at the end of the book of council minutes; another recorded the full text of the ordinance as an entry in the minutes for that session of the council. In order to maintain the archival integrity of the Dutch records these ordinances will appear in their original environment. However, the records in this volume of colonial manuscripts constitute another problem.

When the archivist E. B. O'Callaghan became custodian of the colonial manuscripts in the 1850s, he probably perceived his mission to bring order out of chaos. At that time the records were still in the possession of the secretary of state and stored in the attic of the Albany City Hall. Papers were strewn over the floor and everything was in a deplorable state. O'Callaghan needed an orderly access to these records in order to begin his new career as a translator. His *History of New Netherland* had depended heavily on the unpublished translations of the Dutch records by Francis Adriaen vander Kemp. He had concluded that there were many problems with these translations and that a new translation should be undertaken. While researching land titles among the Dutch records for parties involved in the Rensselaerswijck rent wars, he was forced to confront the Dutch originals and decipher their contents. By 1850 he had acquired such experience and reputation as a Dutch translator that he was selected to translate and edit the documents relating to the history of New York brought back from Europe by John Romeyn Brodhead.

O'Callaghan devoted himself to his new career with diligence and energy. Unfortunately he did not view the records in the attic as a corpus of archival memory. Throughout the centuries they had been moved from the secretary's office in Fort Amsterdam by wagon to Boston during King James II's short-lived Dominion of New England, transported for storage aboard warships in New York harbor during the American Revolution, before finally finding their way to Albany. Each relocation caused further damage to the record books and exposed them to the normal hazards associated with transit; however, what was not damaged or destroyed, at least remained intact in its original context. O'Callaghan, on the other hand, viewed the records primarily as a gold mine of information concerning New York's colonial history under the Dutch, and began preparations to open the mine. The archival integrity of the Dutch archives apparently was of no concern to him. While using Vander Kemp's translations, he was probably annoyed and frustrated by the apparent haphazard organization of the records. For example, in order to search through the minutes of Stuyvesant's council, books B, C, D, E, F, G, H, I, K, P, AA, and DD had to be consulted. O'Callaghan saw no reason to maintain this arrangement, and set about establishing his own organization. The result of his improvement was a series of volumes each containing a type of archival record in chronological order: Volumes I–III, containing secretarial papers, were originally books CC and W; Volumes IV–X, council minutes, were books A, B, C, D, E, F, G, H, I, K, P, AA and DD; Volumes XI–XV, correspondence, were books Q, T, V, X, BB, KK and EE; and Volume XVI constituted books M, N and

LL. This volume is a bit odd because it appears to be a collection of archival types that refused to fit elsewhere. Divided into four parts, part 1 contains laws and ordinances, part 2 Fort Orange records, part 3 Fort Orange records, and part 4 writs of appeal. O'Callaghan then continued this typological scheme with volume XVII, Curaçao papers, books MM and NN; volume XVIII–XXI, Delaware papers, books R, S and FF; volume XXIII, Colve administration, books L, KK and Z. For some unexplained reason O'Callaghan did not assign a volume number to the land papers but retained the Dutch designations of GG, HH and II. The old Dutch record books were torn apart and reassembled according to the above arrangement. Before being rebound in leather bindings, each volume was provided with an introduction and index. This front and back matter supplied by O'Callaghan, including the new leather bindings were all lost in the 1911 State Library fire.

After rearranging the Dutch record books and bundles of papers, O'Callaghan set to work on a guide to the collection, which was published in 1865 as *A Calendar of the Historical Dutch Manuscripts in the Office of the Secretary of State, Albany, New York*. Over the years this guide has been the primary access to the Dutch colonial records. In some cases the chronological entries describing each document are the only information remaining about the contents of pages partly or completely destroyed in the 1911 fire. This guide had become so important to researchers as a quick survey of the Dutch records and the volume and page designations so familiar in scholarly citations that the New Netherland Project decided to maintain the integrity of the guide, as it appeared that the original archival integrity of the Dutch records was beyond recovery. The only alteration made with the present volume has been to group O'Callaghan's part 1 and part 4 together as simply Volume XVI, part 1 in the New Netherland Documents series. Parts 2 and 3, Fort Orange records, are now combined as Volume XVI, part 2, *The Fort Orange Court Minutes*, in the same series.

It is important to remember that the ordinances and writs of appeal in this volume do not constitute the entire body of such records in the Dutch colonial manuscripts. As stated above, additional ordinances or copies of ordinances also appear at the end of some volumes and in others they are incorporated within the minutes of a council session. Until all the volumes of Dutch records have been translated or republished in the New Netherland Documents series, O'Callaghan's *Laws and Ordinances of New Netherland* will have to be consulted for those ordinances appearing elsewhere.

Glossary

aam liquid measure: 37.98 gallons of oil, 40.512 of wine; equal to four *ankers*

anker liquid measure: 10.128 gallons of wine

barrel liquid measure (Dutch *vat*): 226.93 gallons of oil or 243.072 of wine; equal to four hogsheads (*okshoofden*)

burgher a class of citizenship in the community; the *groote burgherrecht* (great burgher right) was purchased for ƒ50, qualifying the holder to serve in administrative offices and on special commissions; the *kleine burgherrecht* cost ƒ20 and served as a license for traders and tradesmen to operate within the designated jurisdiction

can liquid measure: one quart

Carolus guilder equivalent of 1½ guilders

Chalups **(Bay)** Sloop's Bay; alternate name for Oesterbaey

commissary a position appointed by the council on Manhattan to oversee the WIC trading operations at posts such as Fort Orange and to serve as commander of the garrison

court messenger a person appointed by the magistrates to serve court papers on litigants

daalder/daelder equivalent of 1½ guilders

de Jonge junior or the youngest

drieling	inferior beaver pelt; two-thirds of an entire pelt
farmer (of the excise)	the highest bidder for collecting excise taxes on strong drink—payment for this service accrued from whatever was collected beyond the high-bid amount
fathom	linear measure: equal to six feet
fiscal	member of the council on Manhattan in charge of financial matters and law enforcement
florin	synonomous with the guilder; source of the Dutch monetary symbol *f,* referring to the mint in Florence that once produced hard currency for the Habsburg Empire
foot	linear measure: (*voet*) Amsterdam measure equal to 11.143 inches; Rhineland 12.36 inches
gla(e)semaker	glazier
guilder	monetary unit of the Netherlands, consisting of twenty stivers; a common laborer usually earned one guilder per day
harpuys	a mixture of tar, pitch, and resin used for caulking ships
Hellegat	waterway (present-day Hell Gate) between Wards Island in the East River and Long Island, meaning "clear channel"
Heer	lord; a title of high respect
Heeren	the lords; usually in reference to the nineteen directors of the WIC known as the *Heeren* XIX
kill	stream or creek; in the Netherlands it referred to an estuary, as in Sluiskil in Zeeland; no longer an active placename morpheme in Dutch; the word's Dutch origin is rarely recognized by Dutch visitors to New York

last	measure of ship's displacement weight equal to two tons or 4000 pounds
magistrate	local official of the court with executive, legislative and judicial authority; selected by the director general and council on Manhattan from a double list of names submitted by the local court
Manhatans	Manhattan; Algonquin for hilly island
Meester	title of respect for a *schoolmeester*, "schoolmaster,"or short for *heelmeester*, usually a "barber-surgeon"; abbreviated as *Mr.*
mengel	liquid measure: 1.266 quarts of oil or wine; 1.304 quarts of brandy; 1.28 quarts of beer; 1.915 quarts of milk
mudde	dry measure: 4 *schepels* or 3.056 bushels of wheat
mutsje	liquid measure: 2.15 oz.
Nieuwesinckx	a region in New Jersey just west of Sandy Hook later called Navesink by the English
Oesterbaey	Oyster Bay; north shore of Long Island
Oostdurp	East Village; jurisdiction in Westchester
patria	Latin, fatherland; the Dutch use this term often when referring to their homeland
patroon	According to the 1629 "Freedoms and Exemptions" an investor could negotiate for land within New Netherland to establish a patroonship as a perpetual fief, with the obligation to settle fifty colonists within four years
pound Flemish	six guilders
president	Latin, *presens*; the presiding officer or presidnet of a governing board, such as the board of magistrates

Rensselaerswijck patroonship founded by Kiliaen van Rensselaer; approximately the present–day counties of Albany and Rensselaer

rod linear measure: Amsterdam measure equal to 13 *voeten* (12.071 feet); Rhineland 12 *voeten* (12.36 feet)

Roode Hoeck Red Hook; a point of land on the Brooklyn shoreline opposite Governor's Island

schelling six stivers

schepel dry measure: 0.764 bushel of wheat; 1.29 bushels of salt

schepen an elected official of a municipality with administrative and judicial authority

schout an appointed law enforcement officer with the combined duties of a sheriff and prosecuting attorney

sewant wampum in the English colonies; strung pieces of shell with a specific value according to color—six white equal to one purple; as a monetary standard it represented "light money" or 15 stivers to the guilder

stiver monetary unit; $\frac{1}{20}$th of a guilder

Vlissingen Flushing, Long Island

voorlezer lay reader; one who conducts prayer services in the absence of a minister, or who assists the minister by reading portions of the service

Walebocht Wallebout Bay of Long Island in the East River opposite Manhattan, the former site of the Brooklyn Navy Yard, originally meaning Walloon Bay

Key to Abbreviations

LO *Laws and Ordinances of New Netherland*, compiled and translated by E. B. O'Callaghan (Albany, 1868).

NYCD *Documents Relative to the Colonial History of the State of New York*, Vols. I–XI, translated and edited by E. B. O'Callaghan; Vols. XII–XIV, translated and edited by Berthold Fernow (Albany: Weed, Parsons and Company, 1865–1887).

NYCM The "New York Colonial Manuscripts" held by the New York State Archives.

NYHM *New York Historical Manuscripts: Dutch*, Vols. I–III, *Register of the Provincial Secretary*; and IV, *Council Minutes*, translated and edited by A. J. F. van Laer; Vols. V, *Council Minutes*; XVIII–XXI, *Delaware Papers*; GG, HH and II, *Land Papers*, translated and edited by Charles T. Gehring (Baltimore: Genealogical Publishing Co., 1974–1983).

RNA *The Records of New Amsterdam, 1653–1674*, translated by E. B. O'Callaghan, revised and edited by Berthold Fernow, 7 vols. (New York: The Knickerbocker Press, 1897; reprinted Baltimore, 1976).

WIC The Dutch West India Company.

Laws
1647–1658

New Netherland Documents Series
Volume XVI, part one

[16^1:1]

[RENEWAL OF VARIOUS ORDINANCES NO LONGER OBSERVED]*

The director general and council of New Netherland [send] greetings to all those who hear, see or read this, [and] make known how from time to time various ordinances and proclamations have been enacted and posted by them, aiming at the preservation of good government, order, and the prevention of smuggling. However, because the majority of these have fallen into disrepute as well as disuse by many through connivance and non-execution, therefore, the director general and council have considered it highly necessary to renew some of them, and to bring them back again into memory as a reminder to their good subjects, as they hereby do order and command:

Not to tap on the Sabbath†

First, that no one shall, on the Sabbath of the Lord, during divine service, directly or indirectly be allowed to tap any beer, wine or spirits, or to keep a tavern, according to the proclamations of the last of May 1647, 26 September 1656, and 12 June 1657.‡

Not to keep any taverns after 9 o'clock in the evening

Second, also, that no one shall keep any taverns after 9 o'clock in the evening when the bell ceases to ring, according to the aforesaid proclamation of the end of May 1647.

Not to sell any strong drink to the Indians

Third, that no one shall directly or indirectly sell or give out any strong drink to the Indians, according to the proclamations dated 26 September 1656 and 12 June 1657.§

* Although this document was obviously drawn up much later than 1647, it represents the secretary's attempt to codify various ordinances that needed to be renewed. As many of these ordinances had first been enacted in 1647, this document assumed the first page in the book of laws. See also E. B. O'Callaghan's *Laws and Ordinances*, 342–46 (hereafter cited as *LO*).

† The titles in boldface appear as marginal notations in the original.

‡ See *LO*, 62, 310–11; ordinance for 26 September 1656 no longer exists.

§ Also in *LO*, 61.

Not to damage any fences; to keep them in repair

Fourth, that no one shall climb into any gardens, farmlands or orchards, much less damage the fruits thereof, [or] remove the clapboards or other fences; also, that everyone shall properly fence in his gardens, farmlands or orchards, and lots, which being done and still suffering damage by someone or by someone's animals, [such person] to be brought to justice for it and punished according to the proclamation issued the first of July 1647.*

Not to bring any goods ashore or on board unless the duties thereof are first paid

Fifth, that no one shall be allowed to bring any goods or merchandise from ships to shore or from shore to ship, much less be allowed to export them, without first having them properly recorded, inspected, and paying the customary duties thereon; especially the goods and merchandise going to and coming from Virginia, New England, the Caribbean islands, and other places lying outside this our government; all which must pay 10 percent according to custom and order.

No one to depart without a pass

Sixth, that no persons with any ships or barks shall be allowed to depart without a proper pass; also, that no skippers or bark captains be allowed to transport any persons without a pass, under penalty of the proclamation issued the 4th of July 1647.†

Order concerning construction on lots

Seventh, that everyone shall properly build on the lots granted to and obtained by them, with the prior knowledge of the appointed surveyors, according to the order of the 26th of July 1647.‡

No tapsters allowed to brew

Eighth, that no tapsters shall be allowed to brew and no brewers be allowed to tap; or to sell any beer door to door by the pail, whether it be small or heavy beer, according to the ordinance of the 12th of January 1648, hereafter renewed several times.§

---

*   Also in *LO*, 311; ordinance for September 26 no longer exists.
†   Also in *LO*, 65.
‡   Also in *LO*, 74, where the date reads 25 July 1647.
§   Also in *LO*, 80.

Orders concerning wooden chimneys

Ninth, that, in order to prevent fire and damage within the city of N. Amsterdam, no one shall be allowed to make wooden or plastered chimneys, or repair those already built; also, that all chimneys shall be properly swept and kept clear by statute of the fire wardens, according to the proclamation of the 23rd of January 1648.*

To use no weights or measures except those of Amsterdam

Tenth, to use within this our government no other measure, ell or weight except those of Amsterdam, according to the proclamation of the 10th of March 1648.†

Order against brawling

Eleventh, all brawling, maiming, knife–pulling, and wanton acts are forbidden according to the laudable statutes of the aforesaid city of Amsterdam; and all innkeepers and tapsters remain bound and obligated by oath, to report such brawling, maiming, knife–pulling, and wanton acts immediately to the *fiscal*, upon [pain of] being deprived of his trade and a fine assessed thereon. Amplified on the 15th of December 1657.‡

To do no illicit work on the Sabbath

Twelfth, that no one shall be allowed to fish, hunt, or do any ordinary business on the Lord's Sabbath, much less commit any unlawful acts, upon pain of bodily arrest and arbitrary punishment, according to the proclamations of the 29th of April 1648.§

Not to detain or incite another man's servant or maid

Thirteenth, not to seduce or incite anyone's servants, male or female; or to be allowed to shelter the same longer than 24 hours, as well as fugitives and foreigners, without reporting the same to the *fiscal*, magistrates, or *schouts*; and that all servants, male and female, remain bound to complete and obey their contracts, on pain of arbitrary punishment, according to the ordinance of the 6th of October 1648.**

---

*   Also in *LO*, 82–83.
†   Also in *LO*, 88.
‡   Also in *LO*, 324.
§   Also in *LO*, 98–99.
** Also in *LO*, 104.

No wine or beer to be laid in without notification

Fourteenth, that no brewers, factors, or merchants shall be allowed to send out any unexcised beer or wine, or be allowed to move the same beyond their houses from one cellar to another, without having first recorded the same and receiving for it an excise receipt, on [pain] of forfeiting such wine and beer, and fines imposed thereon by the proclamation of the 8th of November 1648.*

Order for the bakers

Fifteenth, that all bakers shall bake white bread and coarse bread at the [established] weight, and sell it at the established price, or hereafter to be established according to the paucity of grain, pursuant to the order and proclamations repeatedly renewed, the last dated the 26th of September 1656.†

Public highways to be properly maintained

Sixteenth, all streets, paths, and public highways to be properly maintained, put in shape, cleaned, and kept passable, according to the ordinance of the 23rd of May 1650.‡

Order concerning smuggling

Seventeenth, in order to prevent all fraud and smuggling, the director general and council ordered under date 28 August 1651 that all ships and vessels departing from here to the fatherland, Virginia, South River or elsewhere, shall be obligated to take in their full cargo before this city of New Amsterdam; also, provide themselves here with necessary firewood and water, and after their departure from this city, allow no barks, boats, or vessels on board without special prior knowledge of the honorable lord director general, *fiscal*, or whomsoever shall be authorized to do so by the director general and council, on pain as is more fully stated in the aforesaid proclamation.§

Eighteenth,** that no one shall be allowed to gallop or race about with any wagons, carts, or sleighs inside the gates and walls of this city, but

---

* An ordinance for this date is no longer among the records.

† An ordinance for this date is no longer among the records.

‡ An ordinance for this date is no longer among the records; however, its substance does appear in *LO*, 114.

§ Renews ordinance passed August 28, 1651, which no longer exists.

** The remaining renewals appear without headings.

the driver shall walk alongside and not sit thereon, according to the proclamation dated the 12th of July 1657.*

Nineteenth, that no one, upon the arrival of any ships, whether from the fatherland or elsewhere, shall attempt at their first arrival to go on board before and until the letters are delivered to the lord General, under penalty of ƒ25 and [forfeit] of the canoe, boat or scow used to go on board, especially pursuant to the proclamation dated the 12th of June 1657.†

Twentieth, not to come to anchor except at the ordinary anchorage, and not to convey any goods on board or ashore except in daylight, according to the ordinance dated as above.

Twenty-first, no skippers or sailors shall be allowed to bring with them any goods or merchandise under the guise of seaman's freight; in any case not exceeding two months' wages, on pain of confiscation according to the ordinance and proclamation dated the 12th of August 1657.‡

[16^1:5]

[ORDINANCE AGAINST TAPPING AND BRAWLING DURING DIVINE SERVICE]

Petrus Stuyvesant, director general of New Netherland, Curaçao, and the islands thereof, commander-in-chief of the Company's ships and yachts cruising in the West Indies, to all those who shall see this or hear it read, greetings.

Whereas we see and observe by experience the great wantoness in which some of our inhabitants indulge, in excessive drinking, quarreling, fighting, and brawling even on the Lord's day of rest, of which we, God's children, again saw and heard sorrowful examples last Sunday in the vilification of the court, to the reproach and censure of ourselves and our office, to the scandal of our neighbors and finally to the disparagement, indeed, contempt of God's divine laws and ordinances, which command us to sanctify this His Sabbath and day of rest, forbidding all maiming, murdering, and the means and provocations by which the same might arise.

---

*   Also in *LO*, 313; actual date on ordinance is 12 June 1657.

†   Also in *LO*, 313.

‡   Also in *LO*, 314; actual date on ordinance is 9 April 1658.

Therefore, we, with the advice of the former lord director general* and our appointed council, in order, as much as it is possible and practicable for us, to provide herein, and to prevent the curse instead of the blessing of God from falling on us and our good inhabitants, do hereby most earnestly order and command that no brewers, tapsters and innkeepers shall be allowed on the Lord's day of rest, called Sunday by us, before two o'clock if there is no sermon or otherwise before four o'clock in the afternoon, to offer, tap or serve any people wine, beer or strong spirits of any sort, and under any pretext no matter what it may be, except for travelers and day boarders, who may be provided therewith for their needs in their lodgings, on pain of forfeiting their business, and in addition six Carolus guilders for each person found in their houses at that time drinking wine or beer; and likewise, we forbid all innkeepers, tavernkeepers and tapsters, on that day and all other days in the week, in the evening after the ringing of the bell, which will take place around 9 o'clock, to allow any more general drinking, or to tap or serve any wine, beer and strong spirits, except to their own household, travelers and boarders, on the same penalty.

And in order to prevent the all too rash pulling of knives, brawling, maiming and misfortunes following therefrom, we, therefore, pursuant to the laudable statute of the most wise and esteemed council of the city of Amsterdam, do enact and order that whosoever shall in haste or anger draw or cause to be drawn a knife or sword against another, shall immediately incur a penalty of one hundred Carolus guilders, or by failure to pay, to be punished for one half a year's hard labor on bread and water; and if he should injure anyone therewith, three hundred like guilders or to spend one and a half years at the aforesaid labor. And we also charge and order our *fiscal*, lieutenant, sergeants, corporals, as well as burghers, inhabitants and soldiers, to use all opportunities, social calls and appropriate diligence, without any feigning, to confront and uncover the violators hereof in order to prosecute them accordingly.

Thus done in Fort Amsterdam in N. Netherland, the 31st of May 1647.†

---

*   Willem Kieft was director general of New Netherland from 1638–1647.

†   Also in *LO*, 60–62. The first ordinance regarding drawing of knives was issued July 11, 1642; see *LO*, 33.

[16¹:6]

[ORDINANCE AGAINST SELLING ALCOHOL TO THE INDIANS;
TRESPASS; FOR THE PROPER MAINTENANCE OF FENCES;
AND ESTABLISHING AN ANIMAL POUND]

Whereas much strong drink is sold daily to the Indians whereby previously serious difficulties have arisen in this country, and it is necessary
to anticipate it in time; therefore, we, the director general and council of
New Netherland forbid and prohibit all tapsters and other inhabitants
henceforth to sell, give or trade in any manner or under any pretext
whatever any wine, beer or strong drink to the Indians; also, not to let it
be conveyed by the pail and thus give it to the Indians by the third or
fourth hand, directly or indirectly, under the penalty of five hundred
Carolus guilders and, in addition, to be responsible for the calamaties
that might arise therefrom.

Also, everyone is warned against and forbidden from damaging
farmlands, whether fences or crops, and whosoever shall be found to
have damaged the fences or crops of any farmlands, gardens or orchards,
shall forfeit one hundred guilders and, in addition, [receive] arbitrary
punishment.

Also, all inhabitants of New Netherland are charged and ordered to fence
and enclose their farmlands properly so that livestock can do no damage
therein; which livestock, whether horses, cows and especially goats and
hogs, must be watched or kept some place else, where they can cause no
damage, for which purpose the *fiscal*, Van Dijck,* shall construct a
pound in which he may hold the livestock until such time as the damage
has been made good and the fine paid. Let everyone be warned and
protect himself against loss.

Done at Fort Amsterdam in New Netherland, the first of July 1647.†

---

* Hendrick van Dijck was *schout–fiscal* of New Netherland from May 22, 1647
until March of 1652.

† Also in *LO*, 64–65. Selling alcohol to the Indians had been prohibited by
ordinance as early as 1643 and again in 1645. It would be renewed in 1656 within
another ordinance. See *LO*, 34, 52, and 259. Further provisions regarding fences
were given in 1654. See *LO*, 185–86.

[16¹:7]

[ORDINANCE CONCERNING VESSELS AND SMUGGLING]

The honorable lord director general and the lord councilors of New Netherland, Curaçao and the islands thereof, residing in New Netherland, on behalf of their High Mightinesses the honorable lords States of the United Netherlands, his Highness of Orange and honorable lord directors of the Chartered West India Company, do hereby proclaim and order:

1.

That all private yachts, barks, ketches, sloops and vessels under fifty *lasts*, whether Dutch, English, French, Swedish or others, wanting to anchor at Manhattan, shall not seek or have any other roadstead than before the city of New Amsterdam, between the point of the *Kapsken** and the guide-board near the City Tavern, under forfeiture of fifty Carolus guilders for the first time after they have been warned; and the large ships may anchor between the aforesaid point and the second guide-board, standing on the way to Smits Valley, under forfeiture of the same amount.

2.

Also, no skippers, merchants or traders, or ships at their first arrival, may put ashore, remove, transport or transship any merchandise or goods, without the arriving vessels being inspected and the goods reported to the honorable lord general or his honorable deputy.

3.

After sunset and before sunrise no ships may discharge or load, or send off or receive any boat with goods or merchandise, or under any other circumstance, except to convey one of the officers on board or ashore, which must be done before the curfew bell in the evening and after reveille in the morning, and from no other place than in front of or near the shed, under forfeiture of all goods and merchandise found in the boat and also one pound Flemish.

---

*   Little cap or hat, describing the point of land at the tip of Manhattan.

4.

No ships, large or small, shall be allowed to depart without first being inspected and twelve hours' previous notice having been given to, and proper clearance received from the honorable lord General or his deputy, under forfeiture of one hundred guilders.

5.

No skippers, traders or anyone sailing with the ships shall be allowed to conceal, take along or transport beyond the jurisdiction of our government any of the Company's servants, free traders or inhabitants of New Netherland, no matter of what nation or capacity they may be, without a proper pass signed by the dirctor or his deputy, under forfeiture of six hundred guilders.

Thus done in council at Fort Amsterdam in New Netherland, the 4th of July 1647.*

[16^1:9]

[ORDINANCE APPOINTING BUILDING SURVEYORS AND
REGULATING IMPROVEMENT OF LOTS]

Whereas we see and notice by experience the previous disorderliness and continued daily practice in the building and erecting of houses; in the extending of their lots far beyond the survey; in the construction of pigpens and privies along the highways and streets; in neglecting and omitting to build properly on granted lots; the honorable lord director general Petrus Stuyvesant and the honorable lord councilors, in order to present the same in the future, have decided to appoint three building surveyors, to wit: the honorable lord Lubbert van Dincklaegen, the quartermaster Paulus Leendersen, and the secretary Cornelis van Tienhoven, whom we hereby authorize and empower to disapprove of and, in the future, to hinder all improper and irregular constructions, fences, palisades, posts, rails, etc.; therefore, we order and admonish each and every one of our subjects, who from now henceforth are inclined to build in or near the city of New Amsterdam and to palisade gardens or lots, that no one is to attempt to practise or to undertake the same without the

---

* Also in *LO*, 71–72. The smuggling ordinance was further amplified in an ordinance of March 10, 1648; see *LO*, 86–92.

prior consent, notification and approval of the aforesaid appointed building surveyors, under forfeiture of 25 Carolus guilders and the clearing of what has been built or erected. Likewise, we want to have each and every one, who has heretofore received any lots warned and notified to improve their lots properly within nine months from now with good and suitable domiciles according to the ordinance, or in default thereof, such unimproved lots shall devolve to the patroon or proprietor, or to whomsoever it pleases him.

Thus done in court session in Fort Amsterdam, the 25th of July 1647.*

[16^1:10a]

[ORDINANCE AGAINST RETAILING BY BREWERS
AND BREWING BY TAPPERS]

The director and council of New Netherland, having observed that there are brewers in and near the city of New Amsterdam who tap and keep a tavern whereby it can arise and happen that the beer that is brewed and then tapped out is not properly recorded or the established excise paid thereon; therefore, the aforesaid lord general and council, pursuant to the ordinances and customs of Holland, forbid, as they hereby do, that all who brew in and near this city shall not be allowed to tap, keep tavern or sell beer by the pail; also, that no tappers shall be allowed to brew or let others brew for them, under forfeiture of all such beer that shall be found in such breweries or tappers' premises, and, in addition, of being excluded from the trade for [*left blank*] months.

Thus done the 12th of January 1648.†

[16^1:10b]

[ORDINANCE ESTABLISHING FIRE REGULATIONS
IN NEW AMSTERDAM]

The honorable director general of New Netherland, Curaçao and the islands thereof, and the honorable lords councilors having observed and seen by experience that some careless people are negligent in keeping

---

*   Also in *LO*, 74–75. On 9 April 1658 and again on 26 April 1663 the council renewed this ordinance; see *LO*, 343 and 438–39.

†   Also in *LO*, 80–81. This ordinance was amplified and renewed several times; see *LO*, 110, 122, and 343.

their chimneys clean (by sweeping) and do not watch their fires, whereby fire broke out in two houses recently and greater damage is to be expected in the future, especially as the houses here in New Amsterdam are mostly built of wood and covered with thatch; also, there are wooden chimneys in some of the houses, which is also extremely dangerous.

Therefore, the honorable general and lords councilors have considered it advisable and highly necessary to provide herein, whereby the aforesaid lord general and lords councilors proclaim, enact and prohibit, as they hereby do, that henceforth no wooden or plastered chimneys shall be allowed to be built in any houses between the fort and the Fresh Water* and those which already exist shall be allowed to remain standing until further orders and at the discretion of the firewardens; and so that the foregoing shall be well observed, for that purpose are appointed as firewardens: from the honorable council, the commissary Adriaen d'Keyser; from the commonalty, Tomas Hall, Marten Krieger, and Gorge Wolsey, in order to inspect at their pleasure the chimneys in all houses between this fort and the fresh water (standing and located in and around this city) [and] whether the same have been kept clean by sweeping, and if anyone shall be found negligent, every time the aforesaid firewardens pronounce or find the chimneys dirty, a fine of three guilders for every chimney pronounced or found to be dirty shall be paid at once without argument, to be expended for the maintenance of fire ladders, hooks and pails (which are to be procured and acquired at the earliest and most convenient opportunity); and if anyone's house burns or causes a fire, whether it be through negligence or by his own fire, he shall forfeit ƒ25, to be expended as above.

Thus done and enacted in Fort Amsterdam in New Netherland; published the 28th of January 1648.†

---

*   '*t Varse Waeter*. This is a reference to a body of water just north of the Commons in New York City, also called *kalck pond*, a placename which eventually developed into Collect Pond under the English. It was a rather large body of water, which the Dutch thought to be bottomless. The shells left there by the Indians were used to make lime mortar, hence the Dutch placename designation *kalck*, "lime."

†   Also in *LO*, 82–83. On September 28, 1648, the council ordered the firewardens to inspect all chimneys in New Amsterdam and on December 12, 1657, ordered a chimney tax on the city for buying fire buckets; see *LO*, 102 and 363. Each town probably made its own fire ordinances. For example, see *LO*, 326, for Fort Orange and 416 for Wiltwijck.

[16¹:11]

[ORDINANCE REGULATING TAVERNS
IN NEW AMSTERDAM]

Petrus Stuyvesant, director general of New Netherland, Curaçao, etc. and the honorable lords councilors, to all those who read, see or hear this read, greetings.

Whereas we see and experience that our former ordinances enacted against inappropriate drinking to excess, both at night and on the Lord's Sabbath, to the scandal and shame of us and our nation, are not being observed and obeyed according to our intent and meaning, we hereby renew, order and proclaim the same so that they shall henceforth be held, maintained and carried out in stricter observance and execution pursuant to the tenor and content set forth therein.

Meanwhile, the cause and reason why these our good orders and well-intentioned ordinances have not been obeyed according to their tenor and content, are that this manner of business and the profit easily derived therefrom diverts and seduces many from their original and first vocation, trade and business to resort to tavern keeping, so that almost one fourth of the city of New Amsterdam is becoming brandy and beer taverns and tobacco shops, by which excess not only honest occupations and trades are neglected and disregarded, but also the common man and Company's servant are notably corrupted; and what is still worse is that the youth, seeing the improper example of their parents and following [   ] from the path of virtue, is brought up in a totally disorderly manner, from which derives cheating, smuggling and fraud, and the clandestine sale of beer and brandy to the Indians and natives, as daily experience, God help us! shows, from which nothing but new animosities are to be feared between them and us; and, moreover, some honest inns established and licensed for the use and accommodation of travelers, strangers as well as inhabitants, which honestly and sincerely pay their taxes and excise, and own or lease proper houses that carry heavy taxes, are seriously injured in their licensed and lawful business by these underground saloons. Wherein we want to provide according to the demand of affairs, opportunity and our ability; therefore, we the aforesaid director general and council do order and enact on the subject of the tapsters and innkeepers the following regulations and bylaws:

1.

First, that henceforth no new taverns, inns, or saloons shall be opened or established except with special prior knowledge and consent of the director and council, unanimously granted and expressed.

2.

The inns, taverns, and saloons already established, shall be allowed to continue at least another four consecutive years; however, in the meantime they are obligated and bound to provide themselves, as [do] other honest businesses in this place, with proper and civil dwellings for the adornment and esteem of this city of New Amsterdam, each according to his condition, ability and circumstance, pursuant to the ordinance and building regulation made by the director and council with the advice and knowledge of the building surveyor.

3.

That the innkeepers and tapsters, who are permitted these businesses, for certain reasons, for at least another four years, may change their trade; however, he may not convey this his prior business of tapping or keeping tavern to another, or lease or sell his house and dwelling to anyone for this purpose, except with the prior knowledge and full consent and permission of the director and council.

4.

Also, the tavernkeepers and tapsters shall henceforth not be allowed to sell, barter or present to the Indians or natives any beer, wine, brandy or spirits, whether providing such by the first, second or third hand, on pain of forfeiting their business and arbitrary correction at the discretion of the court.

5.

Also, for the prevention of all fighting and mischief, they are obligated to notify the officer immediately if anyone is injured or wounded at their house, on pain of forfeiting their business and one Flemish pound for each hour the wound or injury has been concealed by the tapster or innkeeper.

6.

The ordinances heretofore published against improper carousing at night and immoderate drinking on the Sabbath, shall be obeyed with more strict attention and care; namely, that they shall not keep tavern in the evening after the ringing of the curfew bell, or sell or present any beer or spirits to anyone on Sunday (except for the traveler and boarder) before three o'clock in the afternoon when divine service is over, on penalty established thereto in the ordinance.

7.

Also, they shall be bound not to receive directly or indirectly into their houses or cellars any wine, beer or strong spirits before they are reported at the receiver's office and a permit is obtained for them, on pain of forfeiting their business, beer and spirits, and also a heavy fine at the discretion of the court.

8.

Finally, all innkeepers and tapsters, who are so inclined to continue in their business, shall, within the period of eight days after the publication and posting of this, present themselves and report their names to the director and council; also, while there, solemnly promise to obey at once that which has been enacted on the subject of tapsters and innkeepers, in all its parts, or hereafter may be enacted, and to conduct themselves honestly in their business.

Thus done at a meeting in Fort Amsterdam in New Netherland, the 10th of March 1648.*

[16^1:14a]

[ORDINANCE CONSTRAINING HOGS AND GOATS
IN NEW AMSTERDAM]

Whereas the honorable director general and lords councilors of New Netherland have daily seen and noticed that the goats and hogs here around Fort Amsterdam daily cause great damage in orchards, gardens and other improvements, whereby not only hinderance to the propagation of beautiful orchards and gardens follows but also great injury to many private parties.

* Also in *LO*, 93–96.

Therefore, the honorable lord director general and council, desiring to provide herein, order and proclaim that henceforth no hogs or goats shall be pastured or kept between the fortification of New Amsterdam (or thereabouts) and the Fresh Water,* except within their own enclosures. Also, if goats are found outside the enclosures on this side of the Fresh Water, and beyond the Fresh Water without a herdsman or shepherd, the *fiscal* shall be allowed to seize them, and the honorable lord director and council declare them as a prize. Let everyone be warned hereby and protect himself against loss.

Enacted the 10th of March and publised the 16th of March 1648 in New Netherland.

[16^1:14b]

[ORDINANCE CONCERNING OBSERVANCE
OF THE SABBATH]

Petrus Stuyvesant, on behalf of their High Mightinesses, the lords States General of the United Netherlands, his Highness the honorable lord Prince of Orange, and the honorable lords directors of the General Chartered West India Company, director general of New Netherland, Curaçao and the islands thereof, together with the honorable lords councilors.

Whereas we see and find that, in spite of our well–intended regulations and ordinances, heretofore promulgated for the celebration and sanctification of the holy Sabbath in conformity to God's holy command, they are not observed and obeyed according to our good intent and meaning, but that it is still profaned and desecrated in various ways to the great scandal, offence and reproach of the commonalty and foreign neighbors who frequent this place, as well as to the contempt and disregard of God's holy word and our ordinances emanating therefrom.

Therefore, we, the aforesaid director general and councilors, in order to avert, as much as possible, from themselves and their subjects, God's wrath and punishment, which is to be feared from these and other

* *'t Varse Waeter.* See annotation on page 13 for further information about this early Manhattan landmark. The common pasturing area on Manhattan was just to the south of this body of water. It was customary to allow hogs, goats and other domesticated animals to roam free, foraging for themselves until autumn when they were either slaughtered or sheltered for the winter. At this time the owners identified their animals by distinctive marks clipped in the animals' ears.

misdeeds, do hereby renew and amplify their previous proclamations and ordinances, having for the stricter observation thereof and with the prior notification of the servant of the divine word, deemed it advisable that henceforth one shall preach from the word of God and the usual Christian prayers and thanksgiving offered in the afternoon as well as in the forenoon; for which we request and command that all our officers, subjects and vassals to frequent and attend the same; forbidding in the meantime, in conformity with our aforesaid proclamations, all tapping, fishing, hunting and other usual avocations, crafts and trades, whether it be in houses, cellars, shops, ships, yachts or on the streets and in markets, on penalty of such wares, merchandise and goods or the redemption thereof, plus the sum of ƒ25, to be applied until further notice to the poor and the churches; in addition thereto one pound Flemish to be forfeited by the buyers as well as the sellers, by the lessees as well as the lessors, to be distributed half to the officer and half at the discretion of the court. In like manner, we also hereby prohibit and forbid all persons on the aforesaid day from spending their time, to the scandal and shame of others, in intemperate drunkenness and excess, on pain, if so found, of arrest by our *fiscal* and any higher or lower officer, and arbitrary punishment by the court.

Thus done and, after reconsideration, enacted and published the 29th of April 1648 in New Amsterdam in New Netherland.*

[16¹:16a]

[PROCLAMATION AGAINST SALE OF LIQUOR TO INDIANS]

Whereas it is perceived and seen by daily experience that, although it has been repeatedly forbidden in previous proclamations to tap, give, barter or sell by the third or fourth hand, directly or indirectly, and strong drink to the Indians or natives of this country, still one painly sees every day how the Indians run drunken about the Manhatans; also, that the people who live in remote areas suffer great insolence from the drunken Indians, from which, as before, new misfortunes and wars are to be feared.

---

* Also in *LO*, 98. This ordinance was renewed and enlarged to include ordinary labor and games on October 26, 1656, and renewed again in 1657, 1658, and 1663. See *LO*, 258–59, 310, 344, and 448.

Therefore, the honorable lord director general and lords councilors have deemed it necessary to renew once again the previous proclamation and hereby most strictly forbid, as we hereby do, the giving, bartering or selling of any strong drink, howsoever it may be called, and if anyone is so accused after this date even be it reported by the Indians (who, for important reasons, shall be given credence in such matters), he shall receive in addition to the fine in the previous proclamation, without any dissimulation, arbitrary corporal punishment, because it is better that such ill-willed people be punished than that a whole country and community should suffer through their deeds.

Thus done the 13th of May 1648 at a session in Fort Amsterdam in N. Netherland.*

[16¹:16b]

[PROCLAMATION FOR THE INSPECTION OF CHIMNEYS]

The honorable lord director general and lords councilors of N. Netherland order and command the fire wardens, for the purpose of preventing any calamities from fire, to inspect every house and see whether everyone is keeping his chimney properly cleaned by sweeping; and if found in default thereof to pay a fine of three guilders immediately, to be applied according to the proclamation published on 21 January 1648.

Thus done and ordered in session in Fort Amsterdam in N. Netherland, the 28th of September 1648.†

[16¹:17a]

[ORDINANCE CONCERNING WAGES FOR INDIANS]

Whereas great complaints are daily made by Indians and natives to the honorable lord director general and councilors that some inhabitants of New Netherland employ the natives and use them in their service, and often dismiss them unrewarded after their service is completed, refusing to compensate and pay the Indians for their work, contrary to all public

---

* Also in *LO*, 100. The first ordinance was published on June 18, 1643, followed by one in 1645. Further renewals occurred in 1656, 1657, and 1658; see *LO*, 34, 52, 259, 311, 343.

† This proclamation does not appear in *LO*.

laws; and which Indians threaten, it they are not compensated and paid, to pay themselves, or to avenge themselves by other improper means.

Therefore, the honorable lord director general and councilors, in order to avert and prevent, in good time, as much as possible, all such misfortunes, want to warn all inhabitants, who are indebted to the Indians for wages or otherwise, to pay the same without argument; and if they employ them in the future, they shall be obliged to pay them on the testimony and complaint of the Indians (who, for good reasons, shall be given credence in such matters) on pain of such fines as shall be found proper according to the circumstances of the case.

Thus done in council and published the 28th of September 1648 in N. Amsterdam.*

[16^1:17b]

[ORDINANCE AGAINST SHELTERING AND HARBORING FUGITIVES]

Whereas the honorable lord director general and councilors daily see and observe that some of the inhabitants of New Netherland shelter in their houses and living quarters the Company's servants and other of their servants when the same run away from their lords and masters; also, those coming in from abroad from our neighbors, whereby giving many servants, when they are dissatisfied with their service, the means and the incentive to run away, which occurs daily; and whereas the honorable lord director general and councilors want to prevent and hinder the same as much as possible.

Therefore, the honorable lord director general and councilors hereby notify and warn everyone against harboring and sheltering anyone bound to service, whether to the Company or to other private parties, living here or elsewhere, and against sheltering them no longer than 24 hours at the most; and if anyone is found to have acted contrary hereto, he shall forfeit a fine of ƒ150 as a fine payable to whomever shall make the complaint and it is applicable.

Thus done in session the 6th of October 1648.†

* Also in *LO*, 103, where the addition of the last paragraph was appended by O'Callaghan as it does not appear in the original. No further ordinances occur regarding Indian wages.

† Also in *LO*, 104. The listing of council members, however, does not appear in

[16^1:18]

[ORDINANCE CONCERNING TIMELY BUILDING ON LOTS
IN NEW AMSTERDAM]

Whereas the honorable lord director general and councilors of New Netherland have long before this admonished the commonalty by ordinance about their lots on the island of Manhattan that have been previously laid out too spacious, and larger than can be built upon by some inhabitants; and whereas some persons are desirous to build and there is hardly any place to be found here where a house can be suitably constructed.

Therefore, the aforesaid lord director general and councilors have deemed it advisable to inform everyone, for the last time, to build on their lots properly and sufficiently, or in default thereof the lord director general and councilors shall assign suitable places to people who are desirous to build houses in this city of New Amsterdam, and to allow the present proprietor reasonable compensation for the same, at the discretion of the street surveyor. Let everyone be hereby warned; and if anyone has the intention to build, please register their names at the secretary's office, which being done shall impose proper order thereon.

Thus done in session, and published and posted the 15th of December 1648 in New Amsterdam in New Netherland.*

[16^1:19]

[ORDINANCE TO PREVENT FRAUD OF THE EXCISE]

The director general and councilors of New Netherland, to all those who see this or hear it read, greetings.

Whereas we see and observe by experience that [in spite of] the previous ordinances enacted against the frauds and smuggling that are committed in regard to the beer dispensed by the tapsters and innkeepers, and in spite of our previous ordinance, some few inhabitants still practice tapping and brewing at the same time, whereby not only the customary excise is defrauded, but also other tapsters, who make that their only

---

the original. Previous ordinances had been enacted in 1640 and 1642. This ordinance was renewed in 1658; see *LO*, 24, 32, and 344.

* Also in *LO*, 105. See also ordinance of July 25, 1647 in *Laws and Writs of Appeal*, 12 (hereafter cited as *LWA*).

profession, are injured in their livelihood.

Therefore, in conformity with the public law of the fatherland and with a desire to remedy the same, it has been hereby ordered and ordained that no inhabitants who make a business of brewing shall be allowed to tap, sell or dispense, outside of mealtimes, any beer, wine or spirits, not even to boarders whom they claim go to eat with them, under which guise we notice no mean fraud is committed, for the prevention of one and the other, we order, in addition, that henceforth no beer or wine shall be moved from brewers' cellars or warehouses, or transported and placed in the houses of tappers, unless they have first recorded the same in the secretary's office, and the porters or carriers thereof have taken out the appropriate excise permit for the same, signed by the chief clerk of the secretary, which shall be shown and presented on the same day to our *fiscal* Hendrick van Dijck, or to whomever he shall have authorized in his absence as a substitute; notifying, at the same time, all brewers not to send out any unexcised beer, or to release the same to porters, carriers and tappers, unless an excise permit is first shown to them; on pain of forfeiting the beer and wine, and all implements, whether horses, sleighs or any other instruments by which the same are moved, and arbitrary punishment for those who lend a hand thereto.

Thus done and enacted, after consideration, in session in Fort Amsterdam, this 8th of November 1649.*

[16[1]:20]

[ORDINANCE REGULATING BAKERS]

The director general and councilors of New Netherland, to all those who see, read or hear this read.

Let it be known, that upon the numerous complaints made to us by many of our inhabitants concerning the meagerness of the coarse bread as well as the underweight of the white bread, with which the good inhabitants cannot even be accommodated by the bakers, as a consequence of the Indians or natives of the country buying it from the bakers for strung sewant without examining or questioning the weight or price, which the majority of the inhabitants cannot do for lack of strung sewant; as a result it then follows that the Indians and barbarous natives are furnished the

* Also in *LO*, 110–11. See also documents in *LWA*, 3, and *LWA*, 12, for prior ordinances.

best in preference to the Christian nation from a desire and inclination
for the highest profit.

Therefore, the aforesaid director and councilors, being desirous to provide, in the most proper manner, for the general welfare as much as
possible under existing circumstances, do hereby order and ordain that
henceforth, until our further resolution, no bakers shall be allowed to
bake for sale any fine bolted white bread or cake, or to sell such to the
natives or Christians, on pain of forfeiting all the baked white bread, and,
in addition, fifty Carolus guilders to be applied as is customary; provided,
nevertheless, that no inhabitants are hereby prevented from baking or
having baked such a quantity of white bread for their own household or
for honest meals, as their situation requires; however, their honors of the
court hereby intend to interdict and forbid, as they hereby do interdict
and forbid, the needless consumption and general sale of white bread
and cake to the inhabitants as well as to the natives, in order thereby to
prevent and deter what is committed with regard to the sale of common
bread; and so that neither the good inhabitants nor the natives are
inconvenienced over and under weight, the aforesaid director and councilors order that the bakers, who henceforth make a profession of baking
bread for sale, bake the same either of pure wheat or of pure rye, as they
come from the mill, in weights of eight, four and two pounds, at such
prices as shall be set by their honors of the court from time to time,
according to the value and supply of grain.

Thus done and enacted in session, the 8th of November 1649.*

[16¹:21]

[ORDINANCE TO IMPROVE REGULATION OF THE CURRENCY]

The director general and councilors of New Netherland, to all those who
see or hear this read, greetings.

Whereas we see by experience and have seen for some time the decline
and daily depreciation of the loose sewant, among which many circulate
without holes and half finished, made of stone, bone, glass, mussel shells,
conch shells, even of wood and broken [pieces], from which stem the

---

*   Also in *LO*, 112–13. This ordinance was amended April 14, 1650, for bakers to
bake white bread for the commonalty, but no cakes. See *LO*, 115. Further ordinances
regarding the weight and baking of bread occurred in 1651, 1656, and 1658; see *LO*,
120, 261, and 345.

manifold complaints of the inhabitants that they are unable to go to market with such sewant, nor obtain any commodities, not even a small loaf of white bread or can of beer from the traders, bakers or tapsters for loose sewant.

Therefore, desiring to provide for the promotion of trade and the general welfare of the inhabitants, according to our best knowledge at this time, we have resolved and decided that henceforth loose sewant shall no longer be acceptable, nor valid for payment unless the same has been strung on a cord, as has been the custom previously, in order to prevent hereby the further infringement and importation of all lump and unperforated sewant, so as to prevent any future misunderstandings, we, the aforesaid honorable director and councilors, order that the trade [sewant] shall pass and be valid as payment as beforehand, to wit, six white or three black for one stiver; on the contrary, the poorly strung sewant shall pass as eight white or four black for one stiver.

We hereby order and command everyone to regulate himself according to the tenor hereof; and in case of refusal, to be deprived of their trade and business, and the *fiscal* is hereby ordered upon publication to post and make this known wherever appropriate, [and] also to make every effort to see the same executed and obeyed.

Thus done, reviewed and enacted in session in Fort Amsterdam, this 30th of May 1650 in New Netherland.

[16^1:22]

[ORDINANCE FOR THE FURTHER REGULATION OF THE CURRENCY]

The director general and councilors of New Netherland, to all those who hear, see or read this, greetings.

Whereas we have experience, upon the daily complaints of the inhabitants, that our previous orders and proclamations concerning poorly strung sewant, enacted on the 30th of May 1650, for the convenience and protection of the inhabitants, have not been observed and obeyed according to our good intention and meaning, but that, on the contrary, such payment even for small items is rejected and refused by shopkeepers, brewers, bakers, tapsters, tradesmen and laborers, to the great confusion and inconvenience of the inhabitants in general, there being presently no other currency by which the inhabitants can procure small items of daily trade from one another; therefore, the director and councilors, wishing to provide as much as possible for the convenience and protection of the inhabitants, hereby do order and command that, in conformity to our previous proclamations, poorly strung sewant shall be valid, and accepted by everyone without exception for small and daily necessities and commodities required for the household, as currency to the amount of twelve guilders and below, only in poorly strung sewant; from twelve to twenty-four guilders, half and half, that is to say, half poorly and half well strung sewant; from twenty-four to fifty guilders, one third poorly strung and two thirds well strung sewant; and in larger amounts according to the conditions made between buyer and seller, under penalty of forfeiting six guilders for the first time; by refusal and violation of this for the second time, nine guilders; and for the third time, two pounds Flemish and cessation of his trade and business, pursuant to our previous proclamations.

Thus done and enacted at the meeting of the director and council this 14th of September 1650 in New Amsterdam.*

[16¹:23]

[ORDINANCE REGULATING BREAD AND STRONG DRINK]

The director general and councilors of New Netherland, to all those who hear see or read this, greetings.

Let it be known that today we have received the complaints of the good inhabitants, submitted to us by the representatives† of this place, concerning the excessive exaction and usurious profits imposed by some, regarding both white bread as well as the dispensing of wine, brandy, and spirits by the small measure, by some tapsters and tavernkeepers, and practiced a long time to the great damage and detriment of the commonalty and many private inhabitants, wherein wishing to provide, as much as possible the director and councilors of New Netherland have made with the aforesaid representatives a computation of the present price of bread grain; also, what weight it can produce, as well as the present price of wines, brandies and spirits, and how the same is found

---

* These ordinances regarding sewant appear in *LO*, 115–18. The first ordinance regulating the quality, value and stringing of sewant appeared on April 18, 1641, *LO*, 26. They were reissued in a more detailed form on January 3, 1657, and would be followed by numerous adjustments to the currency; see *LO*, 289–92.

† *gemeents mannen*, municipal officials sworn by oath.

to be excessive by the small measure, with the one and the other increased by more than 100 percent after the initial cost.

Therefore, the director general and councilors in order to prevent such exaction and exhaustive consumption, hereby order and command that the pure white bread as well as the wheat and rye bread shall be baked and sold at its correct weight; namely, the wheat and rye bread as previously ordered and published; the whole loaf, eight pounds; the half loaf, four pounds, which shall be sold, until further orders and a better rate of grain, at fourteen stivers for a whole wheat loaf and at twelve stivers for a whole rye loaf; half [loaves] in proportion. With regard to the white bread: it is hereby ordered that the same shall be baked at its exact and correct weight; namely, whole, half and quarter pound [loaves] at the discretion of the baker, without being allowed to reduce these amounts, and the pound of bolted white bread, made from good and pure wheat, shall be sold from no more than three stivers a pound; those of more or less weight to be calculated in proportion.

Furthermore, whereas the director and councilors have been informed by the representatives as well as by various farmers that some bakers refuse to bake rye bread, and do not hesitate to offer as a reason that they can derive more profit from the white and wheat bread, whereby it comes to happen that not only are many needy inhabitants, who cannot afford white bread, inconvenienced and suffer a lack of bread, but also the farmers cannot sell the rye that they have cultivated and produced to the manifest injury of agriculture and the commonalty, the director and councilors do hereby order and command that for the convenience of the indigent as well as the wealthy, rye bread as well as wheat and white shall be baked, on pain of forfeiting their business and 25 guilders for the first time they are found in violation thereof.

With regard to the wines, brandies and spirits that some tapsters have sold for a long time by the small measure for 10, 12, even 14 stivers for an ⅛th or *mutsie* to the great detriment of the commonalty; therefore, the director and councilors order that a *can* of French wine shall be sold in the taverns for eighteen or twenty stivers, Spanish wine for fourteen or twenty-four stivers, a *mutsie* brandy for no higher than seven stivers; and all this until further order and the occurrence of the rising or falling of the price of wines by the large measure.

And in order to accommodate and oblige the good inhabitants and arriving traders still further, with regard to payment in sewant, and if it is not convenient for the former to lay in wines, brandies and spirits, all arriving traders, Scots peddlers and merchants are permitted until further order to accommodate the commonalty by the small measure without excise for strung sewant, but at a reasonable and civil profit; namely, French wine at twelve stivers, Spanish wine at one *daelder*, brandy and spirits at two and three stivers a quart, solely for the convenience of the settlers who are not tavernkeepers; however, with this understanding that such wines fetched from the merchants by the small measure may not be dispensed by smaller or greater [amounts] by any inhabitants, whatever their capacity or nationality may be, on pain of forfeiting the wine and a fine of twenty-five guilders.

Thirdly, whereas it has been reported to the director and councilors that notwithstanding our previously enacted proclamation and order some brewers are dispensing their brewed beer by the small measure and quart, not only to the damage, injury and detriment of the customary excise but also to the hindrance of business of others who are making a profession of tapping and dispensing by the small measure; and whereas we experience that some brewers are practicing such dispensing by the small measure more securely under the pretense of accommodating the commonalty with small beer, our former orders and proclamations are hereby not only renewed, but in addition all such persons are expressly prohibited from dispensing either good or small beer by the small measure and the pail, under penalty expressed in the previous proclamations. In the meanwhile, so as not to subject the indigent to inconvenience, the director and councilors will, as occasion requires, give permission to some certain inhabitants, carrying the required permit, to lay in small beer without excise, and to dispense the same for a reasonable profit by the small measure.

Thus done, enacted and published in our meeting this 5th of June 1651 in New Amsterdam.*

---

* Also in *LO*, 119–22. This ordinance is a reissue and amplification of several previous price regulating ordinances for bread and liquor, as well as regulations for tapping and brewing; see *LWA*, 22 and *LWA*, 18.

[16^1:26a]

[ORDINANCE REGULATING THE OPERATION OF WAGONS, CARTS, AND SLEIGHS IN NEW AMSTERDAM]

The director general and council of New Netherland do hereby order, for the prevention of accidents, that no wagons, carts or sleighs shall be run, ridden or driven at a gallop within this city of New Amsterdam, but that the drivers and conductors of all wagons, carts and sleighs within this city shall not sit or stand on them; however now henceforth within this city (the broad public highway alone excepted)* shall walk by the wagons, carts or sleighs and so take and lead the horses, on the penalty of two pounds Flemish for the first time, and for the second time double, and for the third time to be arbitrarily punished for it, and in addition to be responsible for all damages which may arise therefrom.

Thus done and ordered in the council of the director general and council of New Netherland, the 27th of June 1652.†

[16^1:26b]

[ORDINANCE AGAINST BOARDING SHIPS ARRIVING AT NEW AMSTERDAM BEFORE THEY ARE REGISTERED]

Whereas the director general and council have certain information and knowledge that, notwithstanding the former order and prohibition issued in the time of the honorable director general Kieft,‡ some inhabitants attempt with skiffs, boats, canoes and other craft, to go on board of ships and yachts arriving from fatherland and elsewhere, before such ships, yachts and barks come to anchor before this city New Amsterdam, according to order, as a result many frauds and much smuggling can arise and have heretofore arisen; [therefore] in order to prevent the same the director and council do order that pursuant to a previous resolution no one, of whatever capacity he may be, shall go with any skiff, boat, canoe or other craft to board any arriving ships, or come ashore with any boat from such ships or yachts, before and until such arriving ships, yachts or barks have anchored before this city New Amsterdam, and have reported to the director general and council from where they are coming and under what commission, on pain of forfeiting such skiff, boat or canoe and two

---

* *De brede heere wech*, now lower Broadway.

† Also in *LO*, 128–29.

‡ Kieft issued an ordinance on April 15, 1638, and the WIC reissued and amplified the ordinance, which was published on June 7, 1638; see *LO*, 10, 13–15.

pounds Flemish to be paid for each person who shall be found to have acted against this [order], and if hereafter it may be discovered that such persons, yachts or canoes have conveyed any goods, packages or parcels to or from such vessels, they shall, in addition to the foregoing fine, be arbitrarily punished according to the circumstances of the case.

Thus done in the council of the director general and council of New Netherland, the 27th of June 1652.*

[16¹:27]

[ORDINANCE REGULATING THE PURCHASE OF INDIAN LANDS AND ANNULLING VARIOUS OTHER GRANTS]

The director general and council of New Netherland, to all who see, read or hear these presents read, greetings.

Whereas it has been learned by experience and deed, that some inhabitants of this province, covetous and greedy of land, have (contrary to the order and intent of the honorable directors of the Chartered West India Company expressed in the charter itself as well as in the exemptions of New Netherland, and also in other subsequent orders and regulations) not hestitated heretofore and still do not hesitate, without the knowledge, order or consent of the aforesaid directors, or their deputies here, to purchase, barter or obtain by gift from the natives, and by virtue thereof to pretend actual and real possession and ownership of many and extensive tracts of land, and then again, contrary to the prohibition of the aforesaid company or other ministers here, to sell and convey to others without making or causing to be made in the office of the secretary of this province, according to the ordinance and edicts, any record of such purchased or sold lands in whole or in part; by which purchase, sale and conveyance of such lands, without the knowledge and consent of the honorable company and its government here, not only are the above mentioned directors injured and wronged in their charter and feudal right of redemption, but also the population, cultivation and planting of farms are delayed and retarded, because such lands have for long years lain, and do still remain wild and waste, without any considerable improvement and settlement having been made thereon by the pretended purchasers and proprietors; besides, there are no lands for sale except at an excessively high price, far above the value and rate at which the director

---

* Also in *LO*, 129–30.

general and council could heretofore obtain them from the natives; indeed, some malicious and evil disposed persons have not hesitated to inform and acquaint the Indians what sum and price the Dutch or whites are giving each other for small lots, whence have resulted within a few years past many irregularities and more are to be apprehended unless some remedy be provided for it in time.

Wherefore the director general and council of New Netherland observing on the one hand the contempt of their well-intended order, and on the other hand the irregularities and pernicious consequences which will follow such purchases and sales and conveyances without the knowledge of the lords patroons and without proper patents from the director and council; therefore the director general and council of New Netherland, after mature deliberation and written communication with the aforesaid directors of the Chartered West India Company, do hereby expressly interdict and forbid all persons, of whatever capacity they may be, directly or indirectly from buying any tracts of land from the natives of this province, much less by virtue of purchase or donation undertake to occupy, or sell or convey them to others, without the previous consent or approbation of the company or its deputy here.

In like manner also, do the director general and council of the company, or their deputy here as aforesaid, pursuant to the order and communications of the aforementioned directors, hereby dissolve, annul and make void all claimed or occupied purchases, sales, patents and deeds signed by order of the director and council and sealed with the seal of the province, of which class are the island in the Hellegat, *Nooten Eylant** opposite the Manhatans, *Roode Hoeck*, both the small Flats on Long Island claimed by the former director Wouter van Twiller; the Great Flat, otherwise The Bay, or Amesfoort Flat with the lands adjacent claimed by Wolphert Gerritsen and Anderies Hudde; the maize land, flat and marshland of Canarisse conveyed by gift of the Indians to Jacob Wolphersen, to the serious damage and prejudice of the new village of Middewout; the lands of Katskil with those opposite, purchased and possessed, against the express command, order and prohibition of the director general and council, by Brant van Slichtenhorst; the lands of the Nieuwesinckx purchased by Lubbert van Dincklaegen; the lands of *Chalupes* and *Oesterbaey*, called Matinnecongh, which the natives maintain were purchased by Govert Loockermans and company;† the

* Nut Island, now Governor's Island in New York Harbor.
† Govert Loockermans was the agent for the Verbrugge trading company of Amsterdam.

lands occupied by Thomas Chambers and lately purchased from Brant Aertsen Slechtenhorst aforesaid, the claim of property in all which said enumerated lands and in still others unknown, wherever located within the limits of this province, whether put forth in virtue of purchase or gift, is declared unlawful, null and void; under condition, however, that to the purchasers or pretended owners, shall be reimbursed and restored whatever they by fair account can show that they have paid and given for said lands, so that the director general and council aforesaid, as representatives of the commissioners of the honorable directors to the Chartered West India Company, do by right of redemption belonging to all patroons, reserve and retain unto themselves the aforesaid lands and all others of that description, and pursuant to the order and instructions of the aforesaid directors, will allot and measure out to all and every person, under proper patent and conveyance, in real and actual property, as much land as the recipient will and can cultivate and settle, on condition that he will renew the fief with the company and have the transfer of the land recorded here in the secretary's office.

And it being further notorious and well known that, by virtue of the above stated claims, some of the above specified lands have been sold and conveyed to others, and therefore occupied, built upon and cultivated, from which possession, though illegally obtained, the director general and council are, nevertheless, not inclined to oust the actual occupant nor to frustrate his labor, but the director general and council hereby ordain and command that such occupants and others, who thus far have no proper patent and deed of the lands they possess and have cultivated, shall give in, within the term of six weeks after the publication and posting of these presents, the quantity and extent of their lands, and petition for and receive a proper patent and deed of the same, signed by the director general, as president, and by the secretary of the province, and sealed with the public seal, on pain of forfeiting his lands and the right of possession he has thereto. Let every one be warned against loss.

Thus done, resolved and enacted in the assembly of the director general and council of New Netherland, this first of July 1652, in New Amsterdam. Resumed and published the 2d of the same month.*

---

*   Also in *LO*, 130–34.

[16¹:31a]

[ORDINANCE AGAINST FIRING AT PARTRIDGES AND OTHERWISE WITHIN THE LIMITS OF NEW AMSTERDAM]

Whereas many guns are daily discharged and fired at partridges and otherwise within the jurisdiction of this city of New Amsterdam and in the vicinity of the fort, by which firing people or cattle could easily be struck and injured, against which practice complaints have already been made.

Therefore, the honorable director general and council, in order to prevent accidents, expressly forbid and prohibit all persons henceforward from firing within the jurisdiction of this city, or near the fort, with any guns at partridges or other game that may by chance fly within the city, on pain of forfeiting the gun and a fine at the discretion of the judge, to be applied one-third to the poor, one-third to the church and one-third to the officer.

Thus done and enacted in Fort Amsterdam, in New Netherland, the 9th of October 1652.*

[16¹:31b]

[ORDINANCE TO PROMOTE INCREASED CULTIVATION AND PLANTING OF GRAIN]

The director general and council of New Netherland observing the population and growth of this province both through procreation and increase, which we must thankfully acknowledge as a special blessing of God, as well as by the arrival of many passengers who have come over within the last two or three years in various ships from the fatherland, and being informed and notified by the last communication from the fatherland that many passengers, both freemen and servants of the honorable company, are again to be looked for with the expected return ships, if God will grant them a safe voyage; and it being the bounden duty of the administration, after invoking and imploring God's blessing, to exert every possible effort for means whereby agriculture may be promoted, in order that their subjects entrusted to their care, being supplied with provisions and necessary maintenance, may not experience any want especially of bread grain.

* Also in *LO*, 138.

Therefore the director general and council being informed and aware thereof through their own observation that many of their subjects apply themselves solely to the planting of tobacco, of which the director general and council neither disapprove nor forbid, but in order to prevent the apprehended scarcity of bread as much as it lies in their power, the director general and council have, for the welfare of the country and for the better support of their subjects, resolved hereby to forewarn, order and command all tobacco planters to plant or sow as many hills of maize, or as much land with peas or other hard grain for bread, as they plant hills or fields with tobacco, on pain of forfeiting fifty guilders to be paid by whomsoever is found to fail herein, the one being not less profitable than the other, besides which, it is at the present time highly necessary. We also command all our officers, and magistrates and especially our provisional *fiscal* to keep close watch and to pay strict attention that this our well-intended ordinance be observed and obeyed, as we consider such necessary for the good of the country and our subjects.

Thus done, resumed and enacted in our council in New Amsterdam, the 20th of March 1653.*

[16^1:36]

[ORDINANCE INCREASING EXCISE TAX ON WINE AND BRANDY]†

The director general and council having considered the low state of the treasury together with the great expenses and charges which the honorable Company has to bear here, beyond the monthly wages and board of its officers, for the civil, ecclesiastical and military administrations which have daily increased because of the growth of the population, the director general and council having, after previous remonstrance and communication made long before this to the commonalty of this city, deliberated on what supplementary means may be considered the least burdensome and injurious to the inhabitants, have found no better, fitter nor easier expedient than the imposition of some tax on the wine, brandy and spirits which can best be spared yet are consumed in this country, at a great profit both by buyers and sellers by the large and small measure; therefore, the director general and council have deemed it proper and necessary to tax wine, brandy and spirits as follows, namely: all wines,

---

*   This renews a previous ordinance of November 8, 1649; see *LO*, 111–12.

†   Another version of this ordinance appears in *NYHM, Council Minutes*, 5:68.

brandies and spirits which from this day forward are laid in and retailed by the tavern keeper, and laid in, consumed or exported from this place elsewhere by any other person, whether officer, inhabitant, or stranger, shall pay, in addition to the ordinary excise paid thereon heretofore: eight guilders on a hogshead of French wine; four guilders on an *ancker* of Spanish wine, brandy and distilled spirits; unless someone imports it here or exports it elsewhere from, then the tax is to be paid and satisfied promptly at the receiver's office, half by the buyer and half by the seller. In order to prevent all frauds, connivance and smuggling, the merchants and factors shall be verbally notified and told by the *fiscal* to regulate themselves accordingly in the sale of their wines, brandies and spirits, and to furnish no wine, brandy or spirits to any person or send off the same elsewhere before and until the same be properly registered and the duty paid thereon. On pain of forfeiting the smuggled wines and a fine five times the value thereof.

Done at New Amsterdam in New Netherland, 26 March 1653.*

[16¹:37]

[ORDINANCE ALLOWING AN INCREASE IN THE PRICE OF WINE AND BRANDY FOR TAVERN KEEPERS]†

Whereas invoices indicate that wines are more expensive in the fatherland than formerly, and as a result the tavern keepers purchase them here at a higher price; and in addition, because of the preceding [ordinance], they are taxed somewhat higher, as may be seen by the tenor thereof.

Therefore, the tavern keepers are hereby permitted to sell French wine at twenty-four stivers, brandy and Spanish wine at fifty stivers, or by the *mutsje* at seven stivers, without being allowed to exceed the aforesaid prices. On pain of forfeiting their business and ten pounds Flemish in addition.

18 August 1653.

---

*   Also in *LO*, 142–43.

†   Also in *LO*, 148. This ordinance was disapproved by the directors at Amsterdam in their letter dated June 5, 1654. They pronounced the ordinance impractical and foresaw the impossibility of executing such a law. The directors also admonished Stuyvesant to adhere to the customs and ordinances of Amsterdam in the future. See *NYCD*, 12:1 and *LO*, 148n.

[16¹:38]

The following ordinances were issued
since the arrival of the secretary
Cornelis van Ruyven, namely,
1653 in November.*

[ORDINANCE FIXING THE PRICES OF IMPORTED GOODS]

The director and council of New Netherland. To all those who shall hear, or see this read, greetings.

Let it be known that in the month of September last past the respective New Netherland colonies and courts and their deputies enacted, published, and posted various orders and regulations concerning the great and excessive expense of all sorts of merchandise, foodstuffs and grains, and workers' wages;† which well-intentioned orders and regulations, published and enacted by previous ordinances, and made known to everyone, the director general and council still expect to be promptly observed and obeyed without any connivance, deceit, or favor, on pain of the fine more fully expressed in the ordinances. But whereas the most recently arrived passengers, merchants and traders have not been informed in advance in the matter of declaring their goods and merchandise, [and] because they have also declared their goods and merchandise according to their previous customs, [and] in addition considering among other things the great risk of the sea, the heavy insurance and the extensive storage of the goods and merchandise in the ships, subjecting them to much leakage and loss; all of which having been considered by the director general and council, they find it here well advised that the merchants could not survive with one hundred percent above the duty on the company's invoice at the present time. Therefore, not to annul absolutely the previously enacted order, the director general and council have for the

* The directors in Amsterdam informed Stuyvesant of Van Ruyven's appointment to the post of secretary of the council in a letter dated July 24, 1653. He came over with a high recommendation, and a monthly salary of ƒ36 and annual subsistence of ƒ200.

† These ordinances do not appear among the records. They may have been sent to the directors of Amsterdam and were consequently disapproved. The directors' letter of March 12, 1654, indicates their displeasure with certain ordinances adopted by the assembly concerning the fixing of prices on merchandise. See *NYCD*, 12:1 for the letter and *LO*, 149 for a translated extract concerning this matter.

present time thought it best and necessary to appraise some goods and merchandise as follows:

One pair of men's shoes, sizes 8 to 12   ƒ3:5
One pair of Icelandic stockings at 36 stivers
One firkin of soap at 20 guilders
One quart of salad oil   ƒ1:10
One pound of candles at 12 stivers
One *ancker* of distilled spirits   ƒ32
One *ancker* of vinegar at   ƒ16
One ell of duffel cloth for Christians not to be priced higher
     than ƒ3:10
One hundred pounds of nails   ƒ30
One *ancker* of Spanish wine   ƒ40
One *ancker* of brandy at   ƒ44
One hogshead of French wine at   ƒ110

What further concerns the goods and merchandise that are neither specified nor appraised herein, and some that cannot be appraised such as assorted linens of Haarlem and Leiden manufacture, cloth, worsted stockings, etc., of which some are finer and better than others; also, all materials and necessities required for farms and households, all too numerous to be specified here, the director general and council order that the authentic invoice of the actual cost of these [items] and of all other merchandise, however they might be named, shall be exhibited and shown to the buyers at their request; and for the present out of consideration of the present dangers and the heavy insurance, the seller shall be allowed to ask one hundred and twenty percent above the first and actual cost and no more, on pain of the fines expressed more fully in the previously enacted ordinances. The director general and council hereby give notice that this order and regulation shall only continue for the present time and until further orders from the fatherland, and no longer.

Thus done at the session of the director general and high council. Done at Fort Amsterdam in New Netherland, this 19th of November 1653.*

* Also in *LO*, 149–151.

[16^1:40]

[ORDINANCE REGULATING MARRIAGE BANNS]

The director general and council of New Netherland, to all who hear or see this read, greetings.

Let it be known that we have been reliably informed by a report from our *fiscal* and others, as well as by open letters dated 18 January 1654 from Graevesande that the magistrates there have undertaken and presumed to post marriage banns publicly concerning persons who both keep a residence here and have kept one a long time in and near the city of New Amsterdam, far beyond the district of the aforesaid village. Whereas such is in direct contradiction to both civil and ecclesiastical order of the United Netherlands, which not only the aforesaid magistrates of Gravesande but also all other colonies within this province are by contract and oath bound to observe. Therefore, the aforesaid director general and council order and notify the aforesaid magistrates of Graevesande and all others within this province, to annul such posting of matrimonial intentions, and on sight thereof to withdraw the same, and in all cases to proceed with and confirm no such marriages, either privately or publicly, before and until such persons, according to the style of the Netherlands, have entered and received their banns and proclamations of marriage where they are dwelling and have resided the last years.

Thus done at the session of the director general and council in New Netherland, dated this 19 January 1654, New Amsterdam.*

[16^1:41]

[ORDINANCE IMPOSING DUTIES ON INDIAN
GOODS, WINES, BRANDY ETC.]

The director general and council of New Netherland, to all those who see or hear this read, greetings.

Let it be known to everyone that according to the general contracts made by the skippers and merchants with the honorable company, everyone is bound to deliver into the company's warehouse the goods they load on board and transport here, and to pay one percent and as much more as the director general and council may have imposed thereon before the arrival of the ships, which one percent the director and council have not

* Also in *LO*, 152.

hitherto collected and also found impossible to record because of the variety of merchandise, besides it might cause some difficulties and more expense even on the necessary merchandise such as stockings, shoes, linen, shirts, cloth, soap and other items; the director general and council experiencing the low state of the treasury, and the necessity of finding some means by which the civil, ecclesiastical and military service may be supported and maintained, have therefore come to the conclusion instead of one percent, which is due from all merchants in general from their cargoes and merchandise, to impose something reasonable and tolerable only on the Indian cargoes and less necessary merchandise, such as wine, brandy, spirits and imported beer and salt, which items although least necessary render the most gain and profit and are usually paid for in cash, so that the merchants and shopkeepers henceforth, instead of one percent on their general cargoes, shall be obliged to pay only on the Indian cargoes and less necessary goods in the manner as follows:

> For one ell of duffels   2 stivers
> For one ell cloth, *dosijntjes* or carpet commonly used by the Indians
>   to make coats   2 stivers
> For one Indian coat made of duffels, *dosijntjes* or carpet   8 stivers
> For one hundred pounds of kettle   *f*3
> For one dozen blankets   *f*4
> For one *ancker* of brandy, Spanish wine or distilled spirits   *f*3
> For one hogshead of French wine   *f*6
> Smaller and larger casks in proportion

> One barrel or a half pipe of imported beer   3 guilders
> For one skipple of salt   20 stivers

Which duty shall henceforth be paid, as the staple right, promptly at the receiver general's office, or at least proper security for the payment shall be given to the satisfaction of the receiver, before the aforesaid and other cargoes shall be removed from the honorable Company's warehouse.

Concerning the remaining goods which are numerous and varied, they are hereby free and exempt until further order and regulation, from the indebted one percent, in order to be, like the other merchandise imported into this province, sold and disposed of to the satisfaction of the trader; but on the merchandise which will be exported or sent out of this province or the government thereof, they shall promptly pay the duty or impost previously placed thereon.

Thus done at the session of the honorable director and high council in Fort Amsterdam, dated 28 January 1654.*

[16¹:43]

[ORDINANCE AGAINST PIRATES, AND TO REQUIRE STRANGERS TO REPORT THEIR ACTIVITIES]†

The director general and council of New Netherland, to all who hear or see this read, greetings.

Let it be known that whereas we have been reliably informed and have actually experienced that some pirates and looters, whose commission and pretext is unknown to the director general and council, have been frequenting Long Island and the mainland between this province and the province of our neighbors; the aforesaid pirates being also, so we have been informed, declared pirates and looters by the neighboring governors and magistrates of New England, thus being denied any shelter, asylum, haven and sanctuary within their jurisdiction, and are accordingly to be considered as fugitives and outlaws from New England; which pirates and looters have not failed to molest and plunder the good inhabitants of this province in the countryside, of which diverse evidence can be seen and heard, both now as well as last year, that such has been committed on various subjects; and whereas the director general and council have been reliably informed that such pirates and looters have been sheltered, accommodated, harbored, aided, and abetted by subjects and inhabitants who have established residences within this province, and are consequently so encouraged and emboldened that some of them have dared not only to frequent, spy and keep watch on the outer villages but even on this city under the guise of travelers; therefore, the director general and council, wishing to provide for the inhabitants to the best of their ability, have considered it highly necessary to enact against the aforesaid the following ordinance and regulation:

The director general and council of New Netherland order and command all their subjects, regardless of what nation they may be, none excepted, not to communicate with such pirates and looters, much less harbor,

---

*   Also in *LO*, 153–55.

†   Other copies of this ordinance appear in *NYCD*, 4:448 and 5:235; for a translation of the latter, see *NYHM, Council Minutes*, 5:126. The unrest and turmoil expressed in this ordinance is a result of the First Anglo–Dutch War (1652–54), whose effects were just then being felt in North America.

conceal or hide them, or to accommodate or provide them with any necessaries; however, if anyone may receive any information, or knowledge of the whereabouts of such pirates and looters or where they may reside or shelter themselves, they are to report the same to the magistrates of the nearest village and court immediately, on pain of confiscation of all one's goods and of being declared an enemy of the state and banished from the country.

Secondly, all magistrates of the respective villages within this province are hereby recommended, each within his jurisdiction, to establish and to maintain such order, watch and place of assembly as they think necessary for the security of the good inhabitants of the aforesaid place, according to the circumstances of the locality; and all inhabitants are hereby ordered and charged promptly and without objection to comply with and obey such orders of the magistrates, and at their command promptly and immediately to pursue, attack and capture, if possible, such pirates and looters, on penalty as written above. In order to encourage the good inhabitants in this their duty, the director general and council promise the sum of one hundred *daalders* for every pirate or looter delivered into the hands of the director general and council or their *fiscal*.

Thirdly, in order that the preceding may be better practised and observed by the good inhabitants of this province, the director general and council order and command that all persons who have no residence within this province of New Netherland and come for shelter in any village or house in this country shall be obliged, when required by the magistrate, officer of the law or any citizen or inhabitant, to show an entry and exit pass from the governor or magistrate from where he comes and where he resides, and if anyone be found without a pass, he shall be examined and heard by the magistrate regarding from where he came and for what purpose and business he has come into the aforesaid province of New Netherland, in order, according to the circumstances and facts of the case, to be so disposed of as shall be found proper; and so that the aforesaid may be better obeyed, all inhabitants are ordered not to lodge any unknown foreigners without first making known to the magistrates or officers of the place the name of such arriving travelers or foreigners, under penalty of *f*24.

Furthermore, in order that everyone may be better, and with more certainty, forewarned of any raid and impending danger, the director general and council order and command that no person shall fire a gun within this province at night between sunset and sunrise on pain of forfeiting one Flemish pound for each shot, unless there is some appearance of danger, in which case everyone is not only permitted but hereby commanded to give an alarm of the perceived danger by firing his gun three times in succession, as quickly as possible. When this alarm, is heard by the nearest watch, village or household, such watch, village or household is hereby commanded to do the same in order, by such means, to make the danger known to all watches, villages and households so that everyone may be on his guard and appear under his authorized officer at the appointed place of assembly.

And, in order that no one may plead ignorance, the director general and council order that this general order shall be sent everywhere throughout this province of New Netherland, so that it may be published, posted and enforced by the magistrates of the respective colonies and villages, and so that the opponents there and elsewhere may be properly proceeded against according to the tenor of this ordinance.

Done at the session of the honorable director general and high council held in New Amsterdam, the 8th of April 1654.*

[16^1:47]

[ORDINANCE CONCERNING THE OPERATION OF THE FERRY]†

To all those who shall see or hear this read, greetings. The director general and high council of New Netherland let it be known that great confusion and disorder prevail more and more among the ferrymen on both sides of the ferry of Manhattan, to the great disservice of the passengers and inhabitants of this province, so that those needing to be ferried across often have to wait whole days and nights, and then not without great extortion of double and even more excessive fares, quarreling and other unmannerly practices, forcing cancellation of their trip to the great expense and detriment of foreigners and the good inhabitants of this province.

Therefore, the director general and high council of New Netherland, wishing to prevent all such confusion and irregularities, henceforth, and for the service of the passengers as well as the inhabitants of this province, order, for maximum service and accommodation and minimum expense, as follows:

* Also in *LO*, 155–58.
† The ferry connected Manhattan and Long Island, following the route now serviced by the Brooklyn Bridge.

First, from now on, no person, no matter his capacity, except for the farmer of the ferry thereto authorized by the high administration, shall be allowed to keep or have any ferry boats to carry over any foreign passengers or inhabitants of this province or livestock, goods or anything else (his own property excepted) on pain of paying one pound Flemish for the first offense, two pounds Flemish for the second, and for the third offense forfeiture of the boat and arbitrary punishment, of which the farmer shall receive one third, the officer one third, and the remaining one third to be at the discretion of the judge; therefore, it is ordered that no one shall keep any boat at the ferry for the purpose of conveying over therewith any persons or goods, his own family and goods excepted, or be allowed to loan it to anyone or hire it out, directly or indirectly, to any other persons, his own family and goods excepted, on pain of the aforesaid punishment.

2.

Second. The farmer shall be bound to keep his ferry constantly provided with proper boats and experienced men, and to maintain on both sides of the river for the passengers and inhabitants of this province a covered shed or shelter to protect them from the rain, cold and so forth.

3.

Also, the farmer shall be allowed to build, for his convenience, a punt to convey across wagons, carts and draft animals, and receive:

For each wagon or cart with two horses or oxen	ƒ2:10:
For a cart or wagon with one horse	ƒ2:00:
For a cart or plow	ƒ1:00:
For a hog, sheep or goat, 8 stivers for two, and 3 stivers for each one above that amount.	
For each man or woman, Indian male or female	ƒ : 6:
For two or more persons, each one	ƒ : 3:
For a child under ten years, half fare.	
For a horse or four-footed horned animal	ƒ1:10:
For a hogshead of tobacco	ƒ :16:
For a barrel of beer	ƒ :16:
For an *anker* of wine or spirits	ƒ : 6:
For a tub of butter, soap or the like	ƒ : 6:
For a *mudde* of grain	ƒ : 4:
and what exceeds that ½ stiver per skipple.	

Bundles of goods and other articles not specified herein are to be agreed upon by the parties proportionally.

4.

Also, the farmer shall not be bound to convey any person over or to carry any goods, unless he so desires, until he has received the specified fee.

5.

Also, the farmer shall only be bound to accommodate passengers for the aforesaid fees on summer days from 5 o'clock in the morning until 8 o'clock in the evening, provided the windmill has not been shut down.*

6.

Also, he shall be allowed to ask for a double charge or ferriage at night, before or after the specified time.

7.

Also, the farmer shall receive regular fees during the winter from 7 o'clock in the morning until 5 o'clock in the evening; however, he shall not be bound, unless he so desires, to convey anyone over in bad weather or when the windmill has shut down as a result of a storm.

8.

Also, no one shall be exempt from paying a fee, whosoever he may be, except for the honorable director general and high council, as well as warrant officers or court messengers or others sent over by the high authorities with a pass from the secretary.

---

* During stormy weather it would have been necessary to shut down the windmills by removing the canvas from the sail frames, indicating conditions too dangerous for the operation of the ferry. The windmills west and southwest of Fort Amsterdam would have been visible from the ferry slip on the Manhattan side (near present-day Fulton Street), serving as an indicator of weather conditions.

9.

In order that no one may plead ignorance hereof, we order and direct the farmer to post a copy of this in plain sight on both sides of the ferry in the ferry houses, because we have deemed such to be for the service of the travelers and the good inhabitants of this province.

In witness whereof we have caused our seal to be appended hereto. Done in Fort New Amsterdam, the 1st of July 1654.*

[16^1:50]

[ORDINANCE REGULATING THE DUTIES OF THE PROVOST MARSHAL]

Ordinance according to which the provost marshal in New Netherland on the island of Manhattan is to regulate himself.

First. The provost marshal shall be obedient and compliant, and must take the oath of allegiance to the honorable director general and high council according to form.

Furthermore, he shall keep his residence in Fort New Amsterdam where he will be assigned quarters; and he will be provided with keys, locks and chains of the prison; and he shall be obligated to take good care to lock up and feed the prisoners in the manner ordered by the *fiscal*.

Also, every morning and evening he is to visit the prisoners, examine the locks and take particular care that no fire, rope, iron or sharp objects be left with the prisoner.

Also, the provost marshal shall not secure anyone with heavier or lighter irons than he is ordered to do by the *fiscal*, unless the prisoner lies in wait for night in order to break out, in which case he shall do his best to maintain security and then report the matter to the *fiscal*.

And, if it happens that a prisoner or prisoners be brought in by *schouts* or ships' captains to the provost marshal to be locked up, he shall have the authority to place the same immediately in confinement; however, he must notify the *fiscal* at the earliest opportunity and deliver in writing the names of the injured parties and of the prisoners.

* Also in *LO*, 162–65 and in *NYHM*, *Council Minutes*, 5:151–53.

Also, the provost marshal may separate and imprison all soldiers whom he finds fighting with unsheathed swords in the fort or on the street.

Also, he shall impose a fine of 2 stivers on all soldiers whom he finds without side arms, or in the evening, after nine o'clock, with candles in their quarters.

Also, the provost marshal shall receive for the incarceration of each soldier 10 stivers, and for each citizen or officer 20 stivers.

Also, for major officers or respectable persons occupying his quarters, 30 stivers, and for the board in proportion, according to the regulation devised thereon.

Also, soldiers who avoid parade, either by leaving too soon or arriving too late, shall not only serve double sentry duty but shall pay the provost marshal a fine of 2½ stivers, and if anyone leaves his weapon unattended on guard duty, it shall be held for safekeeping until it is redeemed with the payment of 2½ stivers.

The provost marshal shall receive twelve stivers per day for the board of a common prisoner, on the condition that he provide them weekly with the equivalent of the ordinary ration allowed by the Company, namely:

1½ lbs. of meat
¾ lb. of bacon
1 lb. of fish
1 gill of oil
1 gill of vinegar
A suitable pottage and a supply of bread per week.

Also, the provost marshal shall not be at liberty to absent himself from the fort at night after the guard is posted, except with the special knowledge of the *fiscal* and by permission of the director general.

And, the provost marshal shall receive for his salary the sum of 24 Carolus guilders per month, payable quarterly, exclusive of his board stipends and extraordinary incomes mentioned above.

And, if it should happen that the provost marshal, with his assistants, is not strong enough to perform his duties because of the strength of hostile forces, in the absence of the *fiscal*, the director general, or, in the absence of the latter, the commanding officer, shall, at his request, detail some soldiers from the guard to enable him to execute his orders.

If the provost marshal arrests one or more soldiers, no person, whosoever he may be, shall oppose him or secure the prisoner, on pain of being punished according to the law.

The provost marshal shall be obligated to assist the *fiscal* in making arrests, inspections and in executing the duties of his office.

Thus done at the session of the honorable director general and high council, 20 August 1654 in New Amsterdam in New Netherland.*

[16^1:53]

[ORDINANCE IMPOSING A TAX ON LAND AND CATTLE]

The director general and council of New Netherland, to all those who see this or hear it read, greetings. Let it be known that during the tenure of their administration, now continued for seven consecutive years, they have constantly and at various times and occasions explained to the representatives of the commonalty of this province of New Netherland the great expenses and charges which the honorable directors have now for about 30 years borne and sustained in supporting various civil, ecclesiastical and military personnel, besides other heavy and excessive outlays in furnishing quantities of munitions, materials and other necessities required for construction and maintaining fortresses and other public works, which expenses have greatly increased from year to year; especially these last two years, for which the director general and council, as representatives of the lords patroons, have not been able to obtain any supplemental funds up to this time except the duties on merchandise which do not amount to a third part of the necessary expenses; consequently, their treasury is depleted and henceforth insufficient to meet any longer the charges growing annually by the increase of population. Although this has been demonstrated with valid and clear reasons to the representatives of the commonalty, up to this date still no subsidies have been obtained, not even the tenths for which all inhabitants of this province have been in arrears for a long time, pursuant to the exemptions and freedoms of New Netherland. Whereas these tenths, with regard both to those of the honorable Company and those inhabitants in the countryside, are difficult to collect and deliver, the honorable director general and council have, pursuant their resolution, adopted on 2 June and revised on 28 August, resolved and concluded to

---

* Also in *LO*, 177–79 and in *NYHM*, *Council Minutes*, 5:168–69.

levy in place thereof an equitable tax on land and horned cattle in the following manner: every morgen of land that anyone claims or is entitled to by virtue of a patent shall pay once annually twenty stivers; and for every head of horned cattle (goats and sheep excepted) above three years of age or thereabouts, twenty stivers; for every head of two years, twelve stivers; for houses and lots granted for building purposes, located in the city of New Amsterdam, the village of Beverwijck, near the ferry and elsewhere, belonging to persons who do not claim or own any land, shall be paid to the General Treasury, once annually, the hundredth penny of the real value. The assessment thereof shall be made and done by a commissioner from the high council and two impartial persons from the respective courts of the aforesaid city and villages, each in his jurisdiction, according to which assessment the vacant lots also shall be conveyed and sold if the present owners and proprietors either neglect or are disinclined to build on the aforesaid vacant lots, in accordance with the printed ordinances.*

Thus done at the session of the honorable director general and high council held in New Amsterdam in New Netherland, 24 August 1654 and revised on 28 August.†

[16^1:55]

[ORDINANCE PROHIBITING SALE OF LIQUOR TO INDIANS]

The director general and council of New Netherland, to all those who see or hear this, greetings.

Let it be know that they see and observe by lamentable experience, notwithstanding their previous and frequently renewed ordinances enacted against the selling or giving of strong drink to the Indians or natives of this country, that many Indians are daily seen and found intoxicated, and while drunk they commit many serious acts of insolence, not only in the countryside, from where various complaints have been brought to us, but also, as our experience proves, many and diverse Indians are

---

* In response to Stuyvesant's suggestion of a tax on unimproved lands in 1652, the directors of Amsterdam responded in a letter dated June 6, 1653, that, after deliberation and correction, they had had such ordinances printed and were sending them for publication and posting in the colony. See *NYCD*, 11: 83; translated extract in *LO*, 182. Neither Stuyvesant's draft copies nor the printed ordinances remain among the records.

† Also in *LO*, 180–81 and in *NYHM*, *Council Minutes*, 5:170–71.

almost daily seen drunk and intoxicated within the city; and whereas up to this time the persons who sell, furnish and give the natives drink cannot be discovered; however, in consideration of the needs of the country, together with the danger that is to be expected therefrom if such selling, furnishing or giving of strong drink to the Indians is not prevented, discovered and punished.

Therefore, the director general and council of New Netherland do hereby expressly forbid the aforesaid selling, furnishing, supplying or giving of any strong drink to Indians either here, in the countryside as well as on the rivers, streams and kills, out of sloops or in any manner or by any means, or by what persons soever the same may be done and practised, not only on the penalty formerly expressed, namely, 500 Carolus guilders, but in addition such persons shall be corporeally corrected and punished at the discretion of the judge. In order to discover and prevent the same more effectively, the director general and council of New Netherland have, with the approval of the commissioners and representatives from the magistracy of this city, deemed it highly necessary that, from this time forward, all drunken Indians shall be arrested and imprisoned, and kept in confinement until they have told and declared who had furnished, sold or given them the drink. Such confessions and declarations of theirs shall, according to the circumstances of the case and the persons, be accepted and believed on that point, and the violators hereof shall, on the declaration of the Indians, be punished according to the ordinance and the exigency of the cases. We order our *fiscal* to have this published and posted in all the usual places as soon as possible, and after the publication and posting to put the same into execution without respect of persons, because we consider such to be for the public service and the peace of the inhabitants, in order to prevent greater dangers and misfortunes.

Thus done at the session of the honorable director general and high council held in New Amsterdam, 28 August 1654.*

* Also in *LO*, 182–85 and *LWA*, 18.

[16¹:57]

[RENEWAL OF THE ORDINANCE
REGULATING TOBACCO]

Renewal of the subsequent orders and regulations on the inspection of New Netherland tobacco by the director general and council of New Netherland, in the presence of the burgomasters of this city of New Amsterdam, done and enacted in the year 1653, the 18th of February.

First. Whereas the inspectors cannot approve the tobacco in the winter months, because it has not for the most part been thoroughly sweated, and cannot be easily handled, the inspectors are ordered not to inspect any New Netherland tobacco in the winter months of December, January and February, unless for urgent reasons with the previous knowledge of the director general and council.

2. Inspectors ordinarily shall not be obliged to inspect any tobacco except on Friday and Saturday, which days the director and council have set aside for that purpose, or in case of the departure of ships for Holland, when inspectors will be obliged to accommodate the buyer and seller daily without delay.

3. The director general and council order for urgent reasons that those who have tobacco to inspect, shall see to it that it is brought before the inspectors in barrels or casks, which tobacco after the inspection shall remain in the barrels or casks at a designated place until the same shall be shipped from here.

All the tobacco which is offered to the inspectors for inspection and judged by them under oath to be unmerchantable tobacco, the inspectors, in order to prevent fraud, shall without connivance or regard to person, immediately burn the same, which they are expressly ordered and commanded to do.

The inspectors shall collect their fixed fees immediately after inspection, and in case any person refuse to pay or pretend to have no money with him, the inspectors may take their fee from the tobacco at the price at which it is sold.

All the barrels or hogsheads coming here with tobacco from Virginia and offered for inspection, the inspectors shall be allowed to unhoop at their discretion so that they may see into the middle of the tobacco (where commonly deception is concealed), which they are expressly ordered to obey so that the buyer is not deceived and unwittingly send on to his principal a bad return as a good one.

Which order and regulation the director general and council of New Netherland order and command the aforesaid inspectors, namely Isaacq de Foreest and Gorge Homs, strictly to observe, and furthermore, to charge all inhabitants who have their residence within this jurisdiction to offer the aforesaid inspectors no manner of obstruction or molestation in the discharge of their office, but, if need be, to lend them every reasonable assistance.

Thus done the 18th of February 1653, New Amsterdam in New Netherland; present: the honorable director general, La Montange, Brian Nuton, Cornelis van Tienhoven, Arent van Hattem, and Marten Crieger, burgomasters.

This has been renewed on the 10th of March 1655, and again published and posted in the presence of Messrs. De Sille, La Montagne and Cornelis van Tienhoven.*

[16^1:59]

[ORDINANCE EXEMPTING JEWS FROM MILITARY SERVICE]

The captains and officers of the militia of this city petitioning the director general and council whether the Jewish nation resident in this city should mount the guard under their militia banners, which being considered and deliberated upon, first, the aversion and disaffection of this militia to be fellow soldiers of the aforesaid nation, and to mount guard in the same guardhouse, and considering that the aforesaid nation is not admitted and counted among the militia in the renown mercantile city of Amsterdam or (to our knowledge) in any other city of the Netherlands, whether in the trainbands or in the general militia guard, but that the aforesaid nation for their freedom in that regard contribute a reasonable sum; the director general and council see fit, in order to prevent further discord, that the aforesaid nation shall remain exempt from general expeditions and guard duties, according to the custom of the laudable government of the famous mercantile city of Amsterdam, on the condition that each male above the age of 16 and under 60 years old shall contribute sixty–five stivers every month for the aforesaid freedom of being relieved of general militia duties; and the militia council is hereby authorized and commanded to

* Also in *LO*, 139–40.

obey the same until further orders from us, and according to the tenor hereof, to collect the aforesaid contribution monthly, and upon refusal to institute proceedings.

Thus done at the session in Fort Amsterdam, dated 28 August 1655.*

[16^1:60]

[ORDINANCE CONCERNING THE IMPROVEMENT AND PRESERVATION OF FENCES]

The honorable lord director general and council of New Netherland hearing daily, to their great regret, serious complaints that posts, rails, clapboards and other fences built by the inhabitants at great expense, difficulty and effort around cultivated land and gardens for the preservation of sown land are being stolen by day and night; in order then to prevent the complete trampling and destruction by animals of what has been sown and planted and is yet to be sown and planted through lack of fencing, which, if not attended to in timely fashion, it is feared will happen, and that this coming winter all land and gardens will be stripped of fencing and what has been sown will come to naught, and consequently there will be no grain to harvest next year in the fields.

Therefore the aforesaid honorable director general and council, in the presence of the burgomasters and *schepenen* of this city, being desirous to provide herein in time, as much as possible, do hereby most expressly warn, and at the same time most strictly command each and everyone, whatever rank or standing they may be, from now henceforth not to strip any gardens, sowed or planted lands of posts, rails, clapboards or other fences, on pain, if anyone be discovered to have taken them away, in whole or in part, that he who will be found to have violated this the first time to be whipped and branded; and for the second offense, punished with the rope until death occurs; without deception or respect to person. And if anyone furnishes information after the date hereof as to who may have robbed any lands or gardens of posts, rails, clapboards or anything else, he shall be given a reward and his name concealed. Let everyone be hereby warned.

Thus done at the session at Fort Amsterdam in New Netherland, the 7th of October 1655, and renewed the 30th of December 1658.†

* See *LO*, 191–92 for another version of this ordinance. For an extensive note on the Jews of Amsterdam and New Netherland, see *LO*, 192–94.

[16¹:61]

[ORDINANCE SETTING THE PRICE OF GOOD NEW NETHERLAND BEER]

The director general and council of New Netherland, having considered on the one side the great, excessive and immoderate profit that the brewers demand for their brewed beers, and on the other side the repeated complaints referred by the inhabitants of this province to the brewers, that, upon the imposition or increase of any taxes, they are making their beers increasingly thinner and poorer, and still demand the same price; indeed, more than before when the grain was more expensive and more scarce than it is now, which tends to the great prejudice of the inhabitants, and only to enrich a few.

Therefore, the aforesaid director general and council do hereby command and order that all brewers within this province, or those who make business of brewing, and transport or sell their beers to others, shall be allowed to sell a gauged tun of good New Netherland beer for no more than twenty guilders, or accept any more, for which they shall be bound to brew good beer no worse than has been brewed up until now.

Thus done at Fortress Amsterdam in New Netherland, the 29th of November 1655.*

[16¹:62]

[ORDINANCE PROHIBITING NEW YEAR AND MAY DAY DISRUPTIONS]

The director general and council of New Netherland, to all those who hear or see this read, greetings.

Whereas experience has demonstrated and instructed that on New Year and May days with the shooting, May pole planting and excessive drinking, besides unnecessarily wasting powder, much drunkenness and other insolences are committed, in addition to other sad accidents leading many times to injuries. Therefore, in order to prevent such in the future the director general and council expressly forbid henceforth shooting and planting of May poles on New Year and May days within this province of New Netherland; also, any noise making with drums or dispensing of

† Also in *LO*, 193.
* Also in *LO*, 203–4, and *LWA*, 3 and *LWA*, 9.

any wine, brandy or beer upon those occasions, and this only to prevent further accidents and trouble, for a fine of 12 guilders for the first time, doubled for the second time and arbitrary punishment for the third time; one third for the officer and one third for the poor and one third for the accuser; furthermore, they order all inferior courts in this province to publish and post this in the usual places and to execute the same promptly.

Thus done at the session of the director general and council at Fort Amsterdam in New Netherland. Dated the end of December 1655, and renewed the 30th of December 1658.*

[16^1:63]

[ORDINANCE ESTABLISHING AN EXCISE ON SLAUGHTERED CATTLE]†

The director general and council of New Netherland, to all those who see this or hear it read, greetings.

Whereas diverse complaints are daily made to them, which experience also confirms that now and then cows, hogs and other livestock are caught in the countryside, slaughtered, and offered for sale by Christians or at least by persons reputed to be Christians, who go under the guise and name of Indians.

Therefore, in order to prevent this as much as possible, the aforesaid director general and council do hereby most expressly prohibit and forbid that henceforth within this city and in any of the other places, villages or hamlets in the countryside belonging to this province any cows, calves, hogs, sheep or goats shall be slaughtered, not even by the owner, unless the owner first enter aforesaid animal, whether ox, cow, calf, hog, goat or sheep, on the same day he intends to slaughter it, with the magistrates of the respective place where he belongs, or with such person as shall be appointed thereto by the magistrates, each in his respective locality, and receive a permit to do so, on pain of forfeiting the slaughtered animal and double its value; for which permit to slaughter the owner shall pay

---

*   Also in *LO*, 205–6.

†   The slaughter excise for New Netherland was copied from the slaughter excise established in Amsterdam in 1645. Amsterdam's excise was fixed at the fortieth penny, or two and a half percent, whereas New Netherland's excise was fixed at five percent. See *Handvesten, etc. van Amstelredam*, 1748 edition, folio I:171, quoted in *LO*, 209.

to the magistrate or the collector, to be appointed by the magistrate for that purpose, for the use of the public, one stiver in the guilder of the true value of each animal, whether ox, cow, calf, hog, goat or sheep. In case of dispute, the value to be determined by the magistrates in their jurisdiction, or their deputies. Which monies shall in each city, village or hamlet be laid up and kept, to be, in time of need, employed and applied for the maintenance and protection of the public interests and the villages, either in the levying of soldiers or purchasing of necessary ammunition according as circumstances shall require. The fines for transgressing this law shall be applied and expended, one-third for the informer, one-third for the officer, one-third for the behoof of the public, as aforesaid.

Thus done at Fort Amsterdam in New Netherland,
18 January 1656.*

[16^1:65]

[ORDINANCE FOR IMPROVED COLLECTION OF DUTIES ON EXPORTED FURS]

The director general and council of New Netherland, to all those who see or hear this read, greetings.

Let it be known that they having experienced the great frauds and smuggling which have for a long time past been committed with regard to the duties on peltries, and imposts heretofore placed on the consumption of wine and beer which are exported, are resolved to publicly let them to the highest bidder in the middle of March, except the duties of the customs and the 8 per cent on the peltries which are sent direct by the return ships to the fatherland. In order to act with more certainty and the better to prevent all fraud and smuggling, the director general and council hereby warn and order all skippers, boatmen, traders and merchants, both inhabitants and strangers, not to embark, transport, carry or remove from this time forth, with yachts, boats, carts, wagons or in any other manner any beavers, otters, bearskins or other peltries, unless such peltries be first regularly entered with the company's commissary, each in his district, and an invoice under his signature of the full quantity thereof, by whom shipped or sent and to whom consigned, be brought to the *fiscal*, on pain of forfeiting the concealed peltries and double the value thereof, whether the skipper or owner even brings them with him

* Also in *LO*, 208–9.

for his own use or as freight for others: hereby not only warning all and every one against loss but also, in addition commanding their *fiscal*, commissary, and other officers strictly to execute this law after the publication and posting thereof, duly to inspect all departing and arriving vessels, boats, carts, or wagons and to proceed against the smugglers as the case may require.

Thus done, enacted and resumed the 27th of January 1656.*

[16^1:66]

[ORDINANCE AGAINST PRACTISING ANY RELIGION OTHER THAN THE REFORMED]

Whereas the director general and council of New Netherland have been reliably informed and apprised that not only are conventicles and meetings held here and there within this province, but also that some unqualified persons in such meetings assume the ministerial office, expounding and explaining the holy word of God without being called or appointed thereto by ecclesiastical or civil authority, which is in direct contravention and opposition to the general civil and ecclesiastical order of our fatherland; besides that, many dangerous heresies and schisms are to be expected from such manner of meetings.

Therefore, the director general and council aforesaid hereby expressly forbid all such conventicles and meetings, whether public or private, differing from the customary and not only lawful but scripturally founded and ordained meetings of the Reformed divine service, as observed and enforced according to the synod of Dortrecht in this country, in our fatherland, and other Reformed churches in Europe, under penalty of one hundred pounds Flemish to be forfeited by all those who, being unqualified, assume, either on Sundays or other days, any office whether of preacher, reader or singer, in such meetings whether public or private, differing from the customary and lawful; 25 like pounds to be forfeited by everyone, whether man or woman, married or unmarried, who is found in such meeings.

However, the director general and council do not hereby intend any constraint of conscience in violation of previously granted patents, nor to prohibit the reading of God's Holy Word, family prayers and worship, each in his household, but all public and private conventicles and

* Also in *LO*, 210–11.

meetings, whether in public or private houses, differing from the oft-mentioned customary and ordained Reformed religion.*

In order that this may be better observed and obeyed in the future, and that no one may claim ignorance of it, the director general and council order their *fiscal*, together with the inferior magistrates and *schouts*, to publish this and have it published everywhere within this province and to act against the contraventors, all the more because we find such to concern the honor of God's advancement of the Reformed divine service and the general peace, harmony and welfare of the land.

Thus done, resolved, reviewed and enacted at Fort Amsterdam in New Netherland, the first of February 1656.†

[16^1:68]

[ORDINANCE CONCERNING REGULATION
OF THE WEIGH HOUSE]

The director general and council of New Netherland, to all those who see this or hear it read, greetings.

Let it be known that whereas the impost master of the weigh house of this city has made various complaints to us that the fees, which rightfully accrue to him from all the goods subject to being weighed or which are to be sold by weight, are significantly abridged, because various goods, subject to being weighed, are transported, shipped, and exported without having been properly weighed, and the weighing fees having been paid.

Therefore, the director general and council do hereby notify, warn and order all burghers, merchants and traders residing in this country, or frequenting this place, that from this time forward no person, of whatever capacity he may be, shall be allowed to weigh, transport, ship or export any goods subject to be weighed, or that are to be sold by weight, exceeding 25 pounds without having first paid the fees for weighing them, according to the ordinance posted in the weigh house, and that as

---

*   In a letter to Stuyvesant dated March 12, 1654, the directors at Amsterdam reiterated their resolve to disallow all petitions for calling a minister other than those of the Reformed religion, in accordance with their custom and that of the East India Company; see *NYCD*, 12:1. Both companies, especially the WIC, were supporters of the Gomarists, who desired to establish the doctrine of the Reformed Church as the national religion.

†   Also in *LO*, 211–12.

often and as frequently they shall be sold, transported or transferred; however, in order to avoid the heavy charges for labor, which might burden the merchandise because of transporting to and from the weigh house, the delivery shall be made from ship to ship or from house to house, provided that, before the transporting or exporting occurs, the impost master be notified of it, and the weighing fees be paid; on pain of forfeiting the wares and merchandise, or the just value thereof, or otherwise at the discretion of the director general and council.

Further, in order to prevent all frauds and smuggling as much as possible, it is hereby expressly ordered and commanded that no person shall keep in his house, warehouse or cellar any weight over 25 pounds, except with the express consent of the farmer. Let everyone be warned hereby and guard himself against loss.

Thus done at the session of the honorable lord director general and council, held at Fort Amsterdam in New Netherland, the 27th of April 1656.*

[16^1:70]

[ORDINANCE CONCERNING FURTHER REGULATION OF THE WEIGH HOUSE]

The director general and council of New Netherland, to all those who see or hear this read, greetings.

Let it be known that they, in order to prevent the complaints of some ill–willed people that no order is observed in this country with respect to weights and measures, have caused to be built and furnished at the order and expense of the honorable lords directors at the chamber of Amsterdam, lords and patroons of this province, a proper weigh house, and in addition to the assized weights, to have an assized skipple and ell kept there, conforming with the weight and length of the city of Amsterdam, according to which every other weight, measure, and ell within this province shall be regulated, observed, and put in practice, on the penalty and fine prescribed by former statutes.

* Also in *LO*, 222–23.

In order the better to bring the same into practice, the director general and council have ordered and enacted, as they hereby do order and enact that from now on all goods and merchandise subject to the measure, whether skipple or weights, which are brought in or out of this city, shall be weighed and measured by the sworn and thereto appointed weigh master and master measurer before such merchandise or goods are brought into this city or exported and carried elsewhere out of it, for which the purchasers and sellers together, or else the purchaser or seller alone, according to the conditions stipulated at the purchase, shall pay as the fee for weighing or measuring as follows:

First concerning the weigh house

| For all sorts of silk goods, spun silk, cochineal, saffron | 15 stivers per cento | indigo, preserves, sugars, Spanish leather, all sorts of spices | 10 stivers |
| tobacco, sarsaparilla, sassafras, ivory, all sorts of dyewood, cotton and cotton yarn, wool and woolen yarn, dried hides, copper kettles, butter and cheese | 5 stivers | dried fish, salted meat, pork, tallow, pitch, sulphur, harpuys*, cordage, lead, iron, copper, raisins, prunes, rice | 4 stivers |

And for all uneven weights above and below one hundred pounds, there shall be paid, from one to 25 pounds, one-fourth; from 26 to 50 inclusive, half fee; from 51 to 75 pounds, full weighing fee. However, if anyone should deliver at the same time to one and the same person more than one quantity of the same sort of goods, all the aforesaid quantities or weights of the one and the other shall be added together and payment made for it according to the product of the whole, and for each lot or

* A mixture of tar, pitch, and resin used for caulking ships.

draft weighed shall be paid ¾ of a stiver.

And all goods subject to be weighed, or that are sold by weight, shall pay the weighing fee as often as they are sold, transported, shipped or exported. However, to avoid the heavy charges for labor with which the goods may be burdened in carrying them to and bringing them from the weigh house, whether by cart, sleigh or boat, the delivery may be made from ship to ship or from house to house, by the shortest and quickest way; provided that before the transportation or export take place, the weigh master be notified of it and the weighing fee; on pain of forfeiting the wares and merchandise or the just value thereof, or otherwise at the discretion of the honorable director general and council.

Also, any wares and merchandise sold by the lot or parcel shall not be delivered before and until they are weighed, but the contracting parties can send for the weigh master, the sales and weights *in loco*, and have the wares and merchandise weighed there and so delivered upon paying the weigh master four guilders per day and the like sum for the use of the scales and weights; but if the buyer or seller have his own scales or weights it will be sufficient to pay only the weigh master.

Exempt from the weighing fee shall only be those goods and merchandise that are brought to, or are received at the weigh house belonging to the honorable company, to this city, to the deaconry and other charitable institutions, being really and truly their property and to be converted to their use; all of which the weigh master shall have to weigh *gratis* and *pro Deo*.

Also, no one shall be allowed to weigh in his house any goods exceeding 25 pounds, on pain as aforesaid, or to keep larger weights in his house, store or cellar, unless by express consent of the impost master, on pain of twenty guilders, those who sell weights excepted.

For the convenience of everyone who wishes to have any goods weighed, the impost master or his collector shall be found in the weigh house, Sundays and feast days excepted, from 7 to 11 o'clock in the morning, from 2 to 6 o'clock in the afternoon from the 8th of April to the 8th of October; and from 8 to 11 o'clock in the morning and from 2 to 5 o'clock in the afternoon from the 8th of October to the 8th of April.

The weigh master shall not be bound to weigh any goods before, after or between the aforesaid hours, but have the freedom to record the weight etc. unless that, whenever the hour arrives to close the weigh house, some goods lie there or are in the act of being weighed, and the seller or buyer or both together offer to pay 12 stivers for keeping open the weigh house, when the weigh master remains obliged to open the place and to weigh the goods.

Also, the impost master of the weigh house shall take care that the scales or balances are kept very clean and free from dirt; in like manner, that the scales are regulated when brought out before they are used; and the same be done to the weigh house itself, and done often.

The director general and council reserve to themselves, with the advice and ratification of the honorable directors, the lords and patroons of this province, to alter, diminish, or to enlarge this regulation according to the circumstances of the time and the condition of affairs.

Thus done in the session of the honorable director general and council held in Amsterdam in New Netherland, the 27th of April 1656*.

[16^1:75]

[MODIFICATION OF THE ORDINANCE CONCERNING COLLECTION OF DUTIES ON EXPORTED SPIRITS]

The director general and council of New Netherland hereby make known that, upon the remonstrance and petition of the Dutch and English merchants frequenting this place concerning the duties imposed on exported wines, beer, and distilled wines and spirits, they have facilitated and moderated one third part in form as follows: that in order not to annul the leasing arrangement, and not to prejudice the farmer, the seller has to pay the farmer one third; the purchaser one third and the remaining third shall be entered as an offset to the farmer, together with the receiver of the director general and council, so that the buyer and seller each individually has to pay the farmer only,

on one tun of beer . . . . f1:00:—
on an *ancker* of brandy, Spanish wine or spirits . . . . . f1: 1:—
on one *ancker* of French or Rhine wine . . . . f :11:—
larger or smaller containers in proportion.

Thus done at the session of the honorable director general and council held at Fort Amsterdam in New Netherland, the 7th of June 1656.†

---

* Also in *LO*, 224–27.
† Also in *LO*, 231. See *LWA*, 34 for earlier ordinance.

[16¹:76]

[ORDINANCE CONCERNING PAYMENT OF THE TENTHS]

The director general and council of New Netherland hereby make known that at various times they have been ordered and instructed by the lords patroons to collect the tenths that both the colonies and private plantations owe, according to their obtained patents and grants, and some have owed for many years already.

Therefore, the director general and council hereby warn everyone, namely, those who are subject to tenths according to patent and deed, that no one undertake to remove cultivated produce, whether it be grain, corn or tobacco, before he has amicably come to an agreement with the director general and council about it for the first and coming year, or has shown his produce to the director general and council or their representatives, in order to select the tenths in conformity to the orders and customs of our fatherland, under penalty of fifty guilders above the just value of the tenths, according to the valuation by impartial persons, to be paid by those who shall be found to have acted contrary thereto.

Thus done at Fort Amsterdam in New Netherland, the 27th of June 1656.*

[16¹:77]

[ORDINANCE CONCERNING THE CLEARANCE OF VESSELS AND EXPORT OF GOODS]

Whereas the director general and council of New Netherland have been reliably informed both by remonstrance of the farmer and by others that now and then some vessels depart from here without asking or receiving a proper pass, as is the custom, and without properly entering their exported goods, such as wines, beers and peltries that are subject to duty, by which first the farmer and then the general welfare of the country has been noticeably defrauded; the aforesaid director general and council, wishing to provide herein in conformity with the orders and customs of our fatherland, do hereby interdict and forbid from this time forward any ships, yachts, barks, ketches or any other vessels, of whatever nation they may be, which cast anchor before or near this city, again to lift the same

---

* Also in *LO*, 232. The tenths were to be distributed among the minister, schoolmaster, and various civil employees. See directors' letter to Stuyvesant dated December 19, 1656, in *NYCD*, 12:45; translated extract in *LO*, 232.

or to sail elsewhere from here, wherever that may be outside or within this jurisdiction, without requesting and obtaining a proper pass from the *fiscal*; under a penalty of 50 pounds Flemish.

In like manner the director general and council also most expressly forbid any person to load on board any peltries, wines or beers, which are subject either to excise or recognition fees, before and until they are properly recorded, and the proper recognition and excise fees have been paid, on pain of forfeiting the smuggled goods and three times their value, to be applied as is proper; hereby not only authorizing but also commanding our *fiscal* to inspect any barks or ships properly before issuing them a pass.

Thus done, resolved, resumed, and published at the session of the director general and council held in New Netherland, 27 June 1656.*

[16^1:78]

[ORDINANCE RENEWING AND AMENDING THE PROHIBITION AGAINST SMUGGLING, AND THE ESTABLISHMENT OF SHIPPING REGULATIONS TO PREVENT SMUGGLING]

Whereas the director general and council of New Netherland are to their regret informed and told of the censure and blame under which they are lying among inhabitants and neighbors because of non-compliance of their previously enacted and frequently renewed ordinances against the importation of contraband and the sale thereof both to Christians and Indians alike, some not only presuming that the director general and council connive with the violators, but even publicly declaring that the aforesaid director general and council have opened up the importation and trade in contraband, which, for that reason, is carried on with uncommon licentiousness and freedom. This has moved the director general and council, and again moves them, to revive and renew the previously enacted ordinances against the importation and sale of any kind of munitions of war, be it to Christians or natives; just as they do hereby revive and renew the aforesaid ordinances in order to prevent all ignorance and exception concerning them, adding to them the following amplification, and have resolved, enacted, and ratified with the prior knowledge and approbation of the lords directors of the Chartered West India Company, that henceforth no person, regardless of his nation or capacity, shall be allowed to bring into the country for his own use or

* Also in *LO*, 233–34.

that of the ship any kind of snaphance or gun barrels, finished or unfinished, not even on the Company's permit, except, according to regulation, a carbine, being a firelock of three to three and a half feet barrel length and no longer; on the penalty as before.

Furthermore, whereas daily experience demonstrates that notwithstanding the general prohibition, much ammunition of war is imported not only from the fatherland by the return ships, but also from other places and especially from Virginia and New England, which cannot be properly rectified unless these vessels as well as ships and barks from the Netherlands are strictly inspected and visited; and according to the general complaints, the frauds and smuggling can hardly be rectified and prevented as long as such ships and barks do not load and unload according to rules and regulations previously enacted for that purpose, which the director general and council do hereby resume, renew and amplify as follows:

1.

That all private ships, yachts, barks, ketches, sloops and vessels, whether of Dutch, English, French, Swedish or any other nationality, desiring to anchor at this island of Manhatans and this city, shall neither seek nor select any other roadstead than before this city of Amsterdam on the East River between the headland and the city gate, and in the North River before and near the beavers' trail,* and at no other place; on pain of paying 25 guilders for the first time, 50 guilders for the second time, to be forfeited after they have been warned.

2.

All ships, yachts, barks, ketches, sloops and other vessels, as previously stated, being thus anchored before this city, and at no other place, shall, before discharging and loading any goods or merchandise, be obliged to present a manifest or invoice of their cargo to the director general or his deputy the *fiscal*, and submit themselves to his inspection both on their arrival and departure, and if he should find any more goods than appear on the submitted inventory, manifest or invoice, such goods, according to customary procedure, shall be declared confiscated by the *fiscal* as prosecutor and guardian of justice, and five times the value of the

---

* *Beverspadt*; probably the trail leading inland from Ahasimus in the former patroonship of Pavonia; now Jersey City, New Jersey.

imported concealed contraband shall be exacted, and on pain of arbitrary punishment according to the published ordinance.

3.

The receipt or delivery of all goods and merchandise, which are delivered on shore or received on board, shall be made and take place, without any exception or deceit of persons, within the limits of this city and in no way beyond the same, and that during daylight hours; forfeiting one quarter part of the discovered goods for the first offense; and, in addition to this, forfeiting the scow, boat or vessel used to unload them for the second offense.

4.

No skippers or anyone sailing with ships, yachts, barks, ketches, sloops or vessels, shall take with them or remove any of the Company's servants, any freemen or inhabitants of New Netherland, regardless of nationality or capacity, without the consent or written permission of the director general or his deputy; on forfeiture of six hundred guilders for each person.

And, in order that no one may claim ignorance of this, the director general and council order and command that this ordinance shall immediately be announced, proclaimed, published and posted there where such announcements, proclamations, publishings and postings are commonly done; furthermore, ordering and commanding the *fiscal* and all other officers to hinder, discover, and execute, with regard to the importation and sale of the aforesaid items, in conformity with this our ordinance, proceeding against and prosecuting the violators and transgressors of it without mercy, connivance, favor, fraud or deception, for we have found such to be appropriate for the service of the country and its inhabitants.

Thus done in the session held at Fort Amsterdam in New Netherland, the 11th of August 1656.*

* Also in *LO*, 236–39. This is an amplification of an ordinance issued February 23, 1645; see *LO*, 47.

[16¹:82]

[ORDINANCE REGULATING FEES PAYABLE AT THE CUSTOM HOUSE AND PUBLIC STORE]

Whereas the director general and council of New Netherland are reliably informed, and told of general complaints about certain fees, which have been exacted up to now without their knowledge, concerning various official documents and salaries relating to commerce, which they intend to rectify, according to the orders and instructions of the honorable lords directors; therefore, the aforesaid director general and council do hereby order that henceforth there shall be paid for a bill of lading:

Of one to six hogsheads of tobacco	12 stivers
Of 7 to 12 hogsheads	18 ditto
Of 13 to 24 hogsheads	24 ditto
Of 25 to as many as shall be shipped	50 ditto
Of one hundred beavers	12 ditto
Of 100 to 200 beavers	18 ditto
Of 200 to as many as shall be packed in one chest	30 ditto
Of one or more chests shipped by the same merchant	50 ditto
For a passport fee to the fatherland, whether for a household or an individual	20 stivers
And for the church	40 stivers

Concerning the laborers' wages for bringing the goods and merchandise from the ship to the Company's warehouse, the aforesaid director general and council order that the skippers shall henceforth be obliged to deliver the goods and merchandise at the headland or at the main bank at high tide, in front of or near the Company's warehouse, from where the sworn laborers shall bring them into the Company's warehouse, and receive as pay:

For one container or pipe of wine	6 stivers
For one hogshead	5 stivers
For one *aem* of wine or tun of beer	4 stivers
For one half *aem*	3 stivers
For one *ancker*	2 stivers
For one chest of duffel or another of the same size	8 stivers
For one eastern chest* or large trunk	8 stivers
For a case of axes, nails or kettle ware	5 stivers

---

* *Oosterse kist*, literally an eastern chest; a type of steamer trunk associated with traveling to Central Europe, the Levant or even the East Indies.

Other and smaller containers in proportion at the discretion of the *fiscal* or whoever, in his place, is in charge of the warehouse.

After the goods and merchandise have been delivered at the above rates to the warehouse, the merchants may negotiate with the laborers for the best rate possible, according to the remoteness and distance of the places to which they must be brought; and in the event of unreasonableness, then the *fiscal* shall decide the matter, or whosoever, in his place, shall have charge of the warehouse as commissary. However, no one is to be hindered from having his own goods transported from the warehouse by his own workers or servants, with the consent and order as previously stated.

Thus done at the session of the honorable director general and council held at Fort Amsterdam in New Netherland, the 6th of September 1656.*

[16¹:84]

[ORDINANCE ESTABLISHING A WEEKLY MARKET
AT NEW AMSTERDAM]

The director general and council of New Netherland, to all those who shall see or hear this read, greetings.

Whereas diverse goods such as beef, pork, butter, cheese, turnips, carrots, cabbage, and other country produce in quantity, are brought to this city now and then by the country people in order to sell the same here at the waterside, with which they often have to stay for a long time after having arrived here to their great loss, because the commonalty, or a least a majority thereof, who live at a distance from the waterside, are not aware that such items are being brought in for sale, which not only tends to the inconvenience of the burgher but also to the serious damage of the industrious country man who often loses more than he gains in profit from his goods. Wishing to remedy this, the aforesaid director general and council hereby order that henceforth a market shall be held here in this city on every Saturday at the waterside by the house of *Mr.* Hans Kiersteede,† according to which everyone, who has anything to buy or sell, shall have to regulate himself.

---

* Also in *LO*, 249–50.

† Kiersteede was a medical doctor, whose house stood on the corner of what are now Whitehall and Pearl Streets in New York City. Pearl Street, originally called *Op 't Water*, at the waterside, ran along the southern edge of the island.

Thus done at the session of the honorable lord director general and council, held at Fort Amsterdam in New Netherland, the 13th of September 1656.*

[16^1:85]

[ORDINANCE REGULATING THE SOLDIERS AND OFFICERS IN THE DIRECTOR GENERAL'S COMPANY]

Ordinance for the officers and common soldiers of the company of the honorable lord director general, Petrus Stuyvesant.

The director general, Petrus Stuyvesant, as captain of his company, observing that the last issued order, dated 7 October 1655, concerning the appearance before the colors at the beat of the drum, and the posting of and remaining on guard, is not observed and obeyed by the superior and inferior officers as it ought to be, and as is customary in all garrisons; therefore, notifies and commands all officers and soldiers of his company:

1.

That everyone shall, on the roll of the drum, make himself ready to appear fully armed before the colors, and if anyone shall be found absent at the third beat of the drum, he shall forfeit for the first time, as a sergeant six guilders, a corporal or lance corporal four guilders, a cadet or common soldier three guilders; and for the second absence, he shall suffer arbitrary corporal punishment.

2.

Having appeared and entered ranks at the beat of the drum, in proper fashion, no one shall step out of rank or file while standing or marching, or be replaced; also, not discharge his weapon while standing or marching, without the express order from the captain lieutenant of the unit, on pain of forfeiting one month's pay.

* Also in *LO*, 251.

3.

Those who have guard duty shall, in proper fashion, appear in their own person fully armed at the beat of the drum, perform parade, and continue and remain on guard without being allowed to accept another as replacement, unless with the knowledge and consent of the director general, the captain lieutenant or whomsoever may assume these positions in his absence, on penalty of a half month's pay for the first time, twice as much for the second time, and for the third time an arbitrary corporal punishment. In order that this may be better understood and obeyed, the sergeant of the guard shall not be allowed to leave the fort or the guard except with the previous knowledge and consent of the director general, captain lieutenant or ensign; the corporal, lance corporal or cadet except with consent of the sergeant; no common soldier except with consent of the sergeant, or in his absence, of the corporal, and then only in a small number of two to three at the most at one time, upon penalty as stated above.

4.

No one shall come to guard duty drunk or be allowed to drink while standing guard, on penalty of one *daelder* and as much more as a replacement shall earn who is commanded and brought in his place to the guard by the captain lieutenant or sergeant.

5.

When appearing for parade, they shall appear with their hand and side weapons, and musket rests; with their muskets properly loaded, as in duty bound.

6.

With experience showing that whenever some soldiers are suddenly and unexpectedly commanded to duty, they then complain, and it is also found, that they have no powder or lead; therefore, everyone is hereby notified and expressly ordered henceforth not to discharge his musket either within or outside the fort, except by consent of the lieutenant, ensign or in their absence, of the sergeant, who is hereby ordered and commanded to pay strict attention to it, on pain of forfeiting six stivers for each shot fired without the previous knowledge and awareness of the aforesaid officers; once a week and no more (unless otherwise required because of dampness or foulness of the small arms) the muskets are to be properly loaded with powder and shot and discharged outside the fort along the river's edge, in order to prevent any mishap.

7.

In order the better to prevent the waste of powder and lead, the superior and lesser officers, in particular the sergeants, are ordered every evening at parade to inspect the bandoleers of those having guard duty, and if anyone is found not to have in his bandoleer 6 to 8 full measures of powder and ball, he shall forfeit 12 stivers, and explain where the powder has gone and pay for it.

8.

The sergeant in charge of the parade and the guard shall every morning, whenever the weather is dry and suitable, properly drill the soldiers and the guard detail at least for one hour or half an hour.

The fines shall be applied, one third to the officer or person making the complaint, two thirds to the benefit of the officers and common soldiers of the company.

Thus done at Fort Amsterdam in New Netherland, the 20th of September 1656.*

[16^1:89]

[ORDINANCE REGULATING THE RATES AT WHICH BEAVER
IS TO BE RECEIVED IN PAYMENT OF DUTIES]

Whereas, for a long time now, the payment of the export duty, both on peltries and tobacco, has been very bad, and such that when the honorable company's receiver wishes to make purchases for the company, with the same beavers that some merchants are in the habit of paying to the company, the pay is refused by others, indeed, by the very same persons from whom those beavers have been received, to the serious loss and damage both of the company and of its officials in this country, because some merchants in packing, lay aside the poorest and worst beavers for the company, or else, in case the company or its officials have need of

---

*   Also in *LO*, 252–54.

any supplies, these are charged to them in ordinary settlement fifty per cent or more than they can be obtained by others with good prepared beavers, whereby the Company's treasury in general is greatly retarded, and its officials seriously defrauded.

The director general and council wishing to provide herein as much as possible, have hereby resolved to order and command their *fiscal* and the provisional receiver, not to receive for the export duty any other payment than good, whole merchantable beavers; in no case, any summer skins or *drielingen*,* which the merchants themselves generally refuse and reject; and that at eight guilders per beaver for exported merchandise. Concerning the remitted four percent, which must be paid in silver coin in the fatherland, the receiver is ordered to accept it in silver coin according to its value in our fatherland, or in good beavers, the beaver calculated no higher than six guilders, or in goods, in case the company has need of them, at 50 percent advance on the duty, as the company is in the habit of disbursing these to its servants; and in case there be an uneven amount, and that the total is more or less than one beaver, the payer shall be allowed to pay what is less than half a beaver in silver coin, or whole, well-strung sewant, according to its value here; for what exceeds half a beaver, one whole beaver shall be paid to the receiver, provided he return to the payer the surplus in like coin or sewant.

In order to prevent further disputes about half beavers or scraps, the director general and council order that those which are now commonly passed as half beavers, creating many difficulties, and all other scraps that cannot pass for good whole beavers, shall not be entered or even received by the piece, but by weight, the pound calculated at [*left blank*] guilders.

Done at the session held at Fort Amsterdam in New Netherland, the 27th of September 1656.†

---

*   Three-quarters of a beaver, indicating a substandard fur.

†   Also in *LO*, 255–56.

[16¹:91]

[RENEWAL AND AMENDMENT OF ORDINANCES CONCERNING
OBSERVANCE OF THE SABBATH, FURNISHING LIQUOR
TO INDIANS, EXPORTING LIQUOR WITHOUT A PERMIT,
AND REGULATING THE BAKING OF BREAD]*

The director general and council of New Netherland, to all those who
hear or see this read, greetings.

Let it be known that by daily and sad experience it is found that the
previously issued and frequently renewed ordinances and edicts against
the profaning of the Lord's Sabbath; the unseasonable tapping on that
day, and at night after the posting of the guard or the ringing of the bell;
the very dangerous, indeed, damnable sale or bestowal of wine, beer, and
distilled spirits†; the baking and selling of coarse as well as small or
white bread, are, to the dishonor of God, to the serious damage, loss and
disturbance of the peace and quiet of the inhabitants, and to the gross
contempt of the authority and quality of the superior and inferior
magistrates of this province, neither regarded, observed, maintained nor
even enforced according to the good intention of the director general and
council, and as necessity clearly requires; therefore, the aforesaid director general and council, wishing, by virtue of their office, and prompted
by duty and necessity, to provide herein, do renew and enlarge their
previously enacted ordinances and edicts, and hereby prohibit and forbid:

First, all persons from performing or doing on the Lord's day of rest, by
us called Sunday any ordinary labor, such as plowing, sowing, mowing,
building, sawing wood, blacksmithing, bleaching, hunting, fishing, sailing or any other work that may be lawful on other days, on pain of
forfeiting one pound Flemish for each person; much less any lower or
unlawful exercise and amusement, drinking alcoholic beverages, frequenting taverns or tap houses, dancing, playing cards, *ticktacken,
caetsen, balslaen, clossen, kegelen,*‡ going by boat, cart or wagon before,
between or during the Lord's service, on pain of a double fine; in
particular, no innkeepers shall be allowed to set a buffet before, between
or during the sermons, nor be allowed to tap, bestow, give or sell to

---

* For previous ordinances see *LWA*, 17–19 and 22–23.

† The phrase "to the Indians" was inadvertently left out.

‡ These games (in italics) were popular seventeenth-century pastimes, especially
in and around taverns. They can be loosely described as: *ticktack* or *tricktrack*, a
cross between backgammon and checkers; *caetsen*, a sort of handball played in the
open; *balslaen*, a game similar to *caetsen*; *clossen*, bowling; and *kegelen*, nine pins.

anyone any brandy, beer, or distilled spirits, directly or indirectly, on pain of the innkeeper or tapster forfeiting six guilders for each person, and each person found drinking at the aforesaid time, three guilders; likewise, no innkeepers or tapsters shall be allowed to set buffets on Sunday or on any other day that continue on into the night after the mounting of the guard or the ringing of the bell, nor shall anyone be tapped, sold or given any wine, beer or brandy or distilled spirits, on the same penalty; the domestic guest on public business, alone excepted, authorized with the consent and order of the magistrates.

Secondly, with regard to the very dangerous, injurious and damnable sale, bestowal and giving of wine, beer or distilled spirits to the Indians or natives of this country, from which almost as many mischiefs proceed, or at least are threatened and apprehended, as there are drunken Indians, the aforesaid director general and council, renewing and enlarging their previously published edicts, do hereby order and command, that no person, of whatever capacity or profession he may be, shall sell, trade to, bestow, give, furnish or carry or allow to be carried, to or for any Indians, in or out of the house, by land or water, from yachts, barks, boats, or canoes, carts or wagons, by what ever name such vehicles may be called, either directly or indirectly, any beer, wine, brandy or distilled spirits, under penalty of five hundred guilders, and in addition to be arbitrarily punished on the body, and banished from the country. And in order that the same may be discovered, for the better promotion and maintenance of the public peace and quiet, between the good inhabitants of this province and the barbarians, all superior and inferior officers, free or hired servants of the company, and inhabitants of this province are, by their office and fealty, exhorted, required and commanded to aid in preventing, discovering and giving information of such most dangerous and damnable sale or bestowal of wine, beer, or distilled spirits, or, failing therein, to pay half the fine in case it afterward appear, or become known, that they were privy to, or had not informed of, such sale, gift or present of wine, beer, or distilled spirits to any Indians.

Further, the aforesaid director general and council, being credibly informed and told, that wine, beer and distilled spirits, are peddled and retailed up and along the rivers, from up-going and returning yachts, barks, boats, ships and canoes, do hereby not only interdict and forbid such peddling and retailing, but ordain, enact and command that no skippers, sloop owners, canoemen or boatmen, or any other free or bound inhabitants, of whatever name, nation, capacity or occupation they may be, shall from this time forth, either for themselves or for others, embark, load, take with them, in any bark, yacht, boat, canoe, or another vessel, any wine, beer, brandy or distilled spirits in large or small casks, or even in cans, jugs or demijohns, without having first entered the correct quantity with the officer of the place where the wine, beer or distilled spirits, in large or small quantities, are embarked, shipped or loaded, and received from the officer a certificate or permit, on which shall appear the quantity and quality of casks and other measure of the wine, beer or distilled spirits to be taken along, for whom shipped, and to whom consigned, and shall bring back a proper certificate or proof of the delivery to such person, signed by the officer and the receiver thereof at the place of delivery; and all that on pain of forfeiting the concealed wine, beer or distilled spirits, and a fine of five hundred guilders for the first time, and forfeiting in addition, for the second offense, the bark, yacht boat or canoe.

Thirdly, in regard to the baking and selling of coarse and white bread, neither of lawful weight nor at the fixed price, the director general and council renewing and enlarging the previously published order on that subject, do hereby ordain and command that all bakers and all other inhabitants who make a business of baking or selling bread, whether for Christians or barbarians, shall be obliged, as well for the accommodation of Christians as to derive profit thereby from Indians, to bake at least once or twice a week both coarse and white bread, as well for Christians as Indians, of the stated weight and at the price as follows:

The coarse loaf shall weigh,

The double, 8 lbs., and cost	14 stivers.
The single, 4 lbs., and cost	7 stivers.
The half, 2 lbs, and cost	3½ stivers.

The white loaf shall weigh,

The double, 2 lbs., and cost	8 stivers.
The single, 1 lb., and cost	4 stivers.
The half, ½ lbs., and cost	2 stivers.

All bread found to be of less weight or sold at a higher price, without the previous knowledge, order and consent of the inferior court, shall be forfeit, and there shall be paid in addition a fine of twenty-five pounds Flemish for the first time; for the second time, double as much, and for the third time, six hundred guilders, and their trade be absolutely prohibited.

Further, no bakers or persons who make a business of selling coarse or white bread to Christians or Indians, shall be allowed to mix any sifted bran either wholly or in part with the coarse bread, but bake the coarse bread as the flour comes from the mill; or to make any other sort of coarse or white bread either for Indians or Christians, than is herein previously specified, on the aforesaid penalty. The inspection thereof remains subject to the respective courts, each within its jurisdiction, and those whom, as better judges of bread, they shall adjoin to themselves.

Fourthly, the director general and council, being further informed and considering, that frauds can creep in, both in the matter of tapping and baking, for the concealment whereof excuses may be set up and invented, because no guild or association is hitherto known; to prevent such, as much as possible, the director general and council ordain and command that, from this time forward, no person shall make any profession of baking or tapping unless he first apply to the court in the respective jurisdiction and receive from it, or its agent, a license for that business, which all tavernkeepers and bakers shall renew every quarter of a year commencing the first of November, next and pay for it each time one pound Flemish for the benefit of the respective court, on pain of suspension of his business for notorious and obstinate neglect.

The fines and amercements specified above are to be applied one-third for the officer who shall enter the complaint; one-third for the church or the poor; one-third for the public benefit.

In order that all this may be the better known, practiced and obeyed, and that no one pretend ignorance hereafter on this subject, the director general and council do hereby ordain and command that this shall be published and posted everywhere that it is customary to have publication made, and that after publication they be observed and executed without any favor, affection, simulation or respect of persons, as we find such to be for the public service and for the better and greater peace of the good inhabitants.

Thus done, renewed and amplified in the session of director general and council of New Netherland, the 26th October, 1656.*

---

* Also in *LO*, 258–63.

[16^{1}:98]

[ORDINANCE REGULATING THE CURRENCY]

The director general and council of New Netherland, to all those who see or hear this read, greetings.

Let it be known that whereas they, to their great regret, are daily informed by their experience, and by the numerous complaints of the inhabitants and strangers importuned, respecting the great, excessive and intolerable dearness of all sorts of necessary commodities and household supplies, the prices of which are enhanced from time to time, principally, among other causes, in consequence of the high price of beaver and other peltries in this country beyond the value, which, by reason of the great abundance of sewant, is advanced, to ten, eleven and twelve guilders for one beaver; and sewant being, for want of silver and gold coin, as yet the most general and common currency between man and man, buyer and seller, domestic articles and daily necessaries are rated according to that price, and become dearer, from time to time; the rather, as not only merchants, but also, consequently, shopkeepers, tradesmen, brewers, bakers, tapsters and grocers make a difference of 30, 40 and 50 percent when they sell their wares for sewant or for beaver. This tends, then, so far to the serious damage, distress and loss of the common mechanics, brewers, farmers and other good inhabitants of this province, that the superior and inferior magistrates of this province are blamed, abused and cursed by strangers and inhabitants, and the country in general receives a bad name, while some greedy people do not hesitate to sell the most necessary eatables and drinkables, according to their insatiable avarice, *viz.* a can of vinegar at 18 to 20 stivers; a quart of oil at 4 to 5 guilders; a quart of French wine at 40 to 45 stivers; a gill of brandy at 15 stivers, and two quarts of home brewed beer, far above its price, at 14 to 15 stivers etc., which the greater number endeavor to excuse on the ground that they lose a great deal in the counting of the sewant; that is partly short and partly long; that they must give 11 to 12 and more guilders before they can convert the sewant into beaver.

The aforesaid director general and council, wishing, therefore, to provide herein as much as lies in their power, have, for the good and advantage of their inhabitants, after diverse serious considerations, propositions and debates held at various times, not been able to discover any better expedient, than to declare sewant a commodity and merchandise in the matter of commerce and wholesale trade; to wit, only among those who import it from abroad, or trade it in this province with Indians for furs;

but inasmuch as, for want of silver and gold coin or other pay, sewant must, in smaller quantities, serve as currency between man and man, buyer and seller the aforesaid director general and council have determined, resolved and ordained, as they do hereby resolve and ordain to rate sewant, and as far as is possible to cause it to be rated at the value of beaver, the beaver being still reckoned, until further order and advice from *patria*, at eight guilders and no higher.

And in order to prevent in future the complaints of miscounting of the sewant, with regard to which no few mistakes have been experienced, to the loss of the honorable company's treasury; also, the taking out of short or long sewant, if it be but good, even and well strung, the director general and council further ordain and command, that, from this time forward, after the publication and posting hereof, sewant shall not be paid out or received, between inhabitants and inhabitants of this province, (even for merchandise or for contracts made before this in sewant), by the tally or stiver, but only by a stamped measure, authorized to be made and stamped for that purpose, by the director general and council, the smallest of which measures shall be five stivers; the whole ten, and the double 20 stivers.

And if it should come to pass that the price of the purchased or sold article should not amount to, or equal half the smallest measure or 2½ stivers, the director general and council, in order to prevent objections and disputes, do order and command that the receiver or the payer, shall satisfy or make up the smallest fraction under or over 2½ stivers, by the tally; each white sewant piece being reckoned at two pennies, and each black one at four pennies.

And in order that no one may plead ignorance hereof, the director general and council order and command that this shall be published, and, after publication, observed, executed and obeyed, everywhere within this province of New Netherland, under a fine of 50 pounds Flemish for the first time, and double for the second time, to be forfeited by such as shall be found, after the publication and posting hereof, to have paid out or received any sewant by the tally, or any other measure than that ordained and stamped by the director general and council; such fine to be applied as it ought.

Thus done in the session of the director general and council held in Fort Amsterdam in New Netherland, the 3rd of January 1657.*

* In a letter to Stuyvesant dated December 22, 1657, the directors indicate their approval of the ordinance on regulating sewant with the provision that it be rated at

[16^1:101]

[ORDINANCE CONCERNING THE FENCING OF PRIVATE LAND,
AND AUTHORIZING THE CUTTING OF FIREWOOD
ON UNFENCED LANDS]

The director general and council of New Netherland, to all those who
shall see or hear this read, greetings.

Let it be known that whereas many complaints have lately been presented
to us of the chopping of firewood and cutting of timber on lands claimed
by diverse of our inhabitants by virtue of patents, the principal reason
and cause of which are that many land-grasping inhabitants of this
province have received, several years ago, many and large tracts of land
by letters patent from the director general and council, on the express
condition to cultivate and improve them, which lands many inhabitants
have, for several years, allowed to lie, and which still lie unfenced,
unimproved, indeed, wild and waste, without making any improvement
or bestowing any labor upon them, merely claiming and retaining them
by virtue of the obtained letters patent. Not only is the honorable
company defrauded and curtailed in its revenue, and the settlement of
the country delayed and postponed hereby, but some of our inhabitants
who seek to earn an honest livelihood for themselves by chopping and
cutting firewood and timber, are frequently prevented and hindered in
their design by those who, by virtue of letters patent, lay claim to such
lands without improving and cultivating them, whence many quarrels
and disputes have, at diverse times and places arisen between inhabitants.

In order to prevent this as much as possible, the aforesaid director general
and council do, therefore, again ordain and command that all those who,
by virtue of patents or deeds, claim any lands, shall properly set off and
fence them in, so that the director general and council as well as the
inhabitants may know and see what lands have been granted and what
remain still to be granted,

And the aforesaid director general and council do hereby declare and
ordain that none of our good inhabitants shall be hindered or prevented
to chop firewood or cut timber on unfenced lands, wherever it shall best
suit the convenience of the inhabitants, on pain of legal proceedings
being instituted against those who will have hindered or prevented the
same.

---

no higher value than in New England. See *NYCD*, 12:69; extract translated in *LO*,
292, and *LO*, 289–92. See *LWA*, 60 for prior ordinance.

Done at Fort Amsterdam in New Netherland,
the 16th of January 1657.*

[16^1:103]

[ORDINANCE REGULATING LICENSES AND EXCISE TAXES FOR TAVERN KEEPERS]

The director general and council of New Netherland, to all those who shall see or hear this read, greetings.

Let it be known that they have been informed and told that diverse persons, within the city as well as in the countryside, in the villages and hamlets of this province, undertake and presume to open taverns, tap houses, and to retail beer and wine by the small measure, and to continue to do so without having applied for, or received any license from us or from those by us authorized, which is contrary to the good order and welfare of our fatherland. In addition to that, such tavernkeepers, tapsters and retailers of wine, beer and distilled spirits are opposed to, and refused to pay and satisfy the usual excise imposed on the consumption of wine and beer.

In order to prevent this, the director general and council of New Netherland do hereby ordain that no person within this province shall attempt to keep any tavern, tap house or peddle any beer, wine, brandy or distilled spirits by the small measure, before and until he has applied to and notified the director general and council, or their deputies, namely, the inferior court of the village to which he is subject, and, in addition, has entered with the farmer or his collector the beer, wine, brandies or distilled spirits to be laid in and consumed by him, and thereon paid, for the behoof of the public, the usual excise imposed thereon by the director general and council and publicly let to the highest bidder, whereof Warnaer Wessels is the farmer for the current year, and Jan Theunissen is, with the consent and approbation the aforesaid director general and council, his collector for the village of Vlissingen, on pain of forfeiting the wine, beer, brandy or distilled spirits and five times the value thereof in case any tavern keepers, tapsters or peddlers are found to have smuggled or laid in any beer, wine, brandy or distilled spirits without entry or excise permit, and 25 guilders additional, for the first offense, to be forfeited by those who attempt tapping or retailing of wine, beer or distilled spirits by the small measure without having requested and

* Also in *LO*, 294–95.

received a permit or a license for it from the director general and council or their qualified subaltern magistrates; the fine to be applied one-third for the officer who shall make the complaint, one-third for the farmer and one-third for the public.

Thus done in the session of the director general and council held in Fort Amsterdam in New Netherland, the 23rd of January 1657.*

[16^1:105]

[ORDINANCE REGULATING ADMITTANCE OF GREAT AND SMALL BURGHERS]

The director general and council of New Netherland, to all those who see this or hear it read, greetings.

Let it be known that they out of consideration of the good and voluntary services, expeditions, watches and other burdens, which the burghers have hitherto done and borne, and in the hope and confidence, which the director general and council still indulge, of their continuance and perseverance therein, have, on the humble petition of the burgomasters and *schepenen*, privileged and favored the burghers and good inhabitants of this city, with a great and small burgher right, as can be more fully seen by the grant of privilege made to the burgomasters and *schepenen*, in amplification of that already bestowed; and whereas, in all beginnings, something or somebody must be the first, so that thereafter a distinction and difference may be made, therefore, also, the necessity of such distinction being founded on reason, in the establishment of the great and small burgher right, whereof the burgomasters and *schepenen* have, by petition to the director general and council, requested further explanation, specification and distinction as to who, and what class are, for the present, to be included in the great, as well as in the small, burgher right, the director general and council of New Netherland, invest, qualify, and favor the great burgher right.

First, those who have been and at present are in the high or upper administration of the country, and their descendants in the male line.

Secondly, all former and actual burgomasters and *schepenen* of this city, their descendants in the male line.

Thirdly, the servants of the God's word, formerly and at present in office,

---

* Also in *LO*, 296–97. See *LWA*, 35 for prior ordinance.

and their descendants in the male line.

Fourthly, the commissioned officers of the militia to the ensign inclusive, and their descendants in the male line. All with this understanding, that the above-mentioned gentlemen and persons, for themselves or their descendants in the male line, have not lost nor forfeited burgher right by absence from the city and by not keeping fire and light; agreeably to the laudable custom of the city of Amsterdam in Europe.

Further, all others who desire and are inclined, or hereafter may be desirous and inclined, to be enrolled in the great burgher right, and to enjoy the privileges and benefits thereof, shall, according to the foregoing grant, apply for the same to the burgomasters and receive it, on paying for it the sum of fifty guilders, Dutch money, or the equivalent thereof.

With the small burgher right are invested and favored,

First, all those who have resided and kept fire and light within the city one year and six weeks.

Secondly, all born within this city.

Thirdly, all who have married, or may hereafter marry native born daughters of burghers, provided that the burgher right be not lost or forfeited by absence from this city, or by not keeping fire and light in conformity as aforesaid.

Further, all others who either now or hereafter will keep any shop, however it may be called, and carry on business within this city or the jurisdiction thereof, shall be bound to apply to the burgomasters for the small burgher right, and pay for it twenty guilders Dutch money, or the equivalent thereof.

All servants of the honorable company under wages, also passengers and newcomers who will settle elsewhere, provided they do so within six weeks, remain alone exempt from applying for burgher right, for the exercise of all sorts of handicraft and the practice thereof.

The moneys arising from the receipt of the burgher right shall be received by the burgomasters, and by them expended principally in the strengthening and fortification of this city.

In order that all this may be the better and more regularly practiced, observed and obeyed, the burgomasters are ordered and authorized to make out, or cause to be made out on the first, and all following occasions, correct lists of those who, according to the tenor hereof, are invested, qualified and favored, either with the great or small burgher right, and of those hereafter who obtain and receive the same, and have a true register made of it, and when done, deliver a copy thereof into the office of the secretary of the director general and council.

Thus done, resolved, resumed and enacted in the session of the director general and council of New Netherland held in Fort Amsterdam in New Netherland, the 2d of February 1657.*

[16¹:108]

[ORDINANCE REGULATING THE INSPECTION OF TOBACCO]

Whereas the frauds committed in the sale and exportation of poor, bad, rotten or withered tobacco have, for a long time past, been publicly known, not only in this country, but diverse complaints have also been presented and made from the fatherland, namely, that now and again quantities of such poor, bad, rotten or mouldy tobacco have been sent over by diverse traders, factors and agents of good, respectable merchants, and charged in account to the principals at 6 to 7 stivers when it apparently cost here scarcely 2 to 3 stivers, and on arriving cannot realize the ship's freight; to prevent this, then, as much as possible, the director general, the council, and their assistants, have, on the advice and instructions of the honorable directors, considered it right and necessary to subject the Virginia tobacco to inspection as well as that of New Netherland. But as experience has manifested and proved that inspected good tobacco, the hogsheads of which were, according to order, on the purchase and receipt, marked with the customary branding iron, has been subsequently, fraudulently, either changed or mixed with inferior tobacco, and this could again hereafter be done, and the absent merchant be, notwithstanding, defrauded and the inspection and inspector be suspected, the director general, council, and their assistants have for the better information and security of the absent merchant, and to save from censure the inspection and inspector, deemed it best to leave the purchase and receipt of the Virginia tobacco free and unrestrained, according to the custom of our fatherland, to the buyer and seller, as they shall agree together in regard to the quality of the tobacco and the value of the wares to be exchanged for it, the same rule to apply to the New Netherland tobacco, in case parties can agree together of the delivery thereof. But if

---

* Also in *LO*, 301–3. See NYCM, 8:436 for the ordinance establishing the great and small burgher right; translated in *LO*, 298–300.

they wish to export it to Holland, then the one as well the other will have to be examined and inspected by a proper, trustworthy and sworn person, in or in front of the company's store, before it is embarked or shipped. And although the inspector cannot judge, much less know at what price the tobacco is bought or received, or at what price it is brought into account with the principals, yet he can judge of the comparative quality and grades of goodness. It is, therefore, as already stated, thought best and most proper, provisionally until further advised and instructed by the honorable directors, for the better information and security of the absent merchant, that three sorts, or distinctions of tobacco be made by the inspector, and inspected and marked in this manner, namely:

The best sorts or hogsheads:
V. G. which shall signify Virginia Good;
or N. G. New Netherland Good.

The next sorts:
V. M. or N. M. and shall signify Virginia or New Netherland Merchantable tobacco.

The third sort:
V. S. or N. S. and shall signify Virginia or New Netherland Poor tobacco.

The last sort, which may not even be considered poor, shall be marked with a **0** or [*left blank*], and shall not be embarked, or exported except on the shipper's own account, on condition that, before shipping here, he give sufficient security for the ship's freight and other charges, if it happen, as is reported, that such condemned tobacco might not realize in the fatherland the freight and other charges.

In order to prevent further loss to the skippers or merchants, and to protect the honorable company's store from blame, also to give still more light both to the directors and merchants, it is further resolved and ordained that, as the shipped tobacco is inspected and marked according to the decision of the inspector, even so shall it be specified and designated in the bills of lading and invoices by the inspector's brands, in addition to the merchant's marks; and all this until further and better regulation, as circumstances and experience shall require.

Meanwhile, are all persons forewarned and cautioned not to ship any Virginia, or New Netherland tobacco before and until the same be examined, inspected and marked or branded, in accordance with the tenor hereof, by the inspector to be appointed and sworn for that purpose, on pain of forfeiting one pound Flemish for every hogshead, to be paid as well by the merchant who shipped it, as by the skipper who received it.

Thus done, in the session of the honorable director general and council held in Fort Amsterdam in New Netherland, the 30th of March 1657.*

[16¹:112]

[ORDINANCE RENEWING REGULATIONS CONCERNING OBSERVANCE
OF THE SABBATH; SELLING LIQUOR TO INDIANS
AND SMUGGLING; ANCHORAGE POSITIONS;
DELIVERYOF MAIL; UNSAFE DRIVING]

The director general and council of New Netherland, to all those who see, or hear this read, greetings.

Whereas it is seen and found by experience, that our previously enacted and frequently renewed ordinances and edicts against the desecration of the Lord's Sabbath; against tapping and setting buffets after the ringing of the evening bell at nine o'clock; against the sale of strong drink, either wine, beer or distilled spirits to Indians in houses, or out of yachts, barks, sloops, canoes, or on shore along the rivers; against exporting or importing diverse merchandises, either out of or into this province, without these having been duly entered, whence arise considerable frauds and smuggling; against anchoring, discharging or loading of any ships, yachts or barks, beyond the gates and walls of this city, and the hoist erected for that purpose, and leaving the ship and going on board after sunset and before sunrise; against driving and galloping with wagons, carts or sleighs, have all, and many other well meant enacted and repeatedly renewed placards, by lapse of time, fallen into disuse and neglect; indeed, they are not observed and obeyed according to the tenor thereof. Therefore, the director general and council again comprehending the necessity of them, hereby ordain, command and renew:

First, that no person, of whatever rank or nation he may be, shall, within this province, on the Sabbath, or Lord's day of rest, commonly called Sunday by us, or during divine service, entertain any company, or be allowed to buy, sell, give or receive, directly or indirectly, under whatever pretext, any wine, beer, or strong drink in any tavern, or perform or carry on any trade or business, much less go or ride for pleasure in boats, carts or wagons, on the penalty and fine heretofore

* Also in *LO*, 307–9. The first ordinance regulating tobacco was issued on August 19, 1638; see *LO*, 16.

affixed thereto, and last renewed and here proclaimed in front of the city hall on the 26th of October 1656.*

Secondly, no person shall, directly or indirectly, within this province under any pretext whatsoever, sell, give, or present to any Indians any wine, beer, or strong drink, either on land or water, from houses, yachts, barks, boats or canoes; which, that it may be the better prevented, no person shall be permitted, in accordance with the previously enacted and renewed ordinance, dated as aforesaid, namely 26 October 1656, to embark, or take with him any wine, beer, or strong drink, in any barks, boats or canoes, not even for his own provision, unless he have previously entered the same with the officer of the place where he embarked it, and that, in its true quantity and quality, on pain of forfeiting what is smuggled, and five times the value thereof, he remaining bound to exhibit, on his return, a receipt of delivery of the entered and embarked liquors, agreeable to the ordinance thereupon published and renewed as aforesaid, dated 26 October 1656.†

Thirdly, the director general and council hereby renew, ordain and command, that no person shall ship or embark, much less carry out of or within this province, any goods or merchandises, of whatsoever nature they may be, without entering the true quantity and quality thereof, and having them inspected according to the entry by the *fiscal*, inspector, or some other official of the director general and council, appointed, or hereafter to be appointed, for that purpose. In like manner, also, no goods or merchandise, coming from without here or elsewhere within this province, shall be discharged, unless their true quantity and quality have been previously entered, on pain of forfeiting the concealed goods. In case the unrecorded or concealed goods are found to be contraband, five times the value in addition. In order to prevent all pleas of ignorance, the director general and council sufficiently warn every one that, in obedience to superior orders, for the purpose of discovering fraud and smuggling, they will exercise, and cause to be exercised, stricter care and attention in the premises, in the searching and examining of ships, barks and yachts, both at this place and also on the way sailing up and down the rivers, when and where they shall think proper, and the opportunity shall present itself.

Fourthly, the director general and council renew and ordain that the common roadstead and anchoring place for all ships, yachts, ketches,

* See *LWA*, 72 for this ordinance.
† *Ibid.*

sloops, barks etc. shall be, on the East River between the hoist and the Capske; on the North River, in front of and near the beavers' trail;* at which roadstead and anchorage all ships, yachts, ketches, sloops, and barks, weather, wind and tide permitting, shall come to anchor and remain lying there during their unloading and loading, without any goods beyond the gates of this city; and that by daylight, between sunrise and sunset, before and after which no goods or merchandises shall be discharged or taken on board, or any boats or scows go or leave the vessel, except by special permission, upon the fine formerly enacted therefor.

Fifthly, the director general and council renew and ordain that no person shall, on the arrival of any ships, whether from fatherland or elsewhere, attempt to go on board at their first coming into port, either while yet under sail or lying at anchor, before or until the *fiscal* or some officer of the director general and council has been on board, and the letters received and delivered to the honorable general, on the penalty of twenty-five guilders. And, whereas by such unseasonable boarding and delivering of letters, many mistakes occur and many complaints are made that letters and invoices are lost, the director general and council ordain that neither the skippers nor the supercargoes shall deliver any letters except such as belong to the director general and council, to any person, before and until a proper list is made of the letters brought with them whether at sea or in port, in order to be sent according to said list to the right man or owner. For the trouble of making out the list and numbering, the ship's supercargo may demand and receive three stivers for each letter.†

Sixthly, and for this time lastly, the director general and council ordain that no person shall gallop or race within the gates and walls of this city with any wagon, cart or sleigh, and no driver shall sit on such wagons, carts or sleighs whether drawn by oxen or horses, but walk alongside the same, and if he shall be caught and found sitting or standing thereon he shall pay a fine of one pound Flemish, and be prohibited from using such wagon, cart, or sleigh and the draft animals thereof for six weeks.‡

In order that all this may be the better known, practiced and obeyed, and that no person may plead ignorance henceforth in the premises, the director general and council hereby order and command that this shall

---

*   *Beverspadt*; see *LWA*, 63.
†   See *LWA*, 63–65 for previous ordinance regarding smuggling.
‡   See *LWA*, 28 for previous ordinance.

be published and posted everywhere that publication is usually made, and observed and executed without any favor or respect of persons, as we find such to be for the good of the country, and for the welfare and greater tranquillity of the good inhabitants.

Thus done and renewed in the session held at Fort Amsterdam in New Netherland, the 12th of June 1657.*

Published and posted on 13 June.

[16^1:117]

[ORDINANCE AGAINST SMUGGLING]

The director general and council of New Netherland, to all those who shall see this or hear it read, greetings.

Whereas it is found more and more every day that great frauds and smuggling are committed and perpetrated by the importation of diverse merchandises under the name and guise of sailors' freight, whereby not only the honorable company is curtailed in its account; the farmer defrauded in his leased excise, inasmuch as such imported goods are most times sold under hand in a clandestine manner; the general merchants who pay the regular duties, are injured in their trade, for they cannot with their goods compete against such imported and smuggled articles; but also the owners and freighter of such ships are themselves wronged out of a great part of their freighted money, as it is confidently presumed and believed that the greater part of such smuggled goods are embarked without their knowledge or consent.

The director general and council of New Netherland wishing to provide herein, hereby order all skippers, ship's officers and sailors not to bring with them any goods or merchandises without exhibiting here a proper list thereof signed in the fatherland, and in all cases, not to exceed two months' wages, which must appear on the invoice, on pain of forfeiting the imported and unrecorded merchandise or goods.

---

* Also in *LO*, 310–14.

Thus done in the session of the honorable director general and council held at Fort Amsterdam in New Netherland, the 12th of August 1657.*

[16^1:118]

[ORDINANCE AGAINST EXPORTING GOODS WITHOUT A PERMIT]

Whereas the director general and council of New Netherland are informed and learn, that the ordinances and edicts heretofore enacted and frequently renewed against the bringing on board and embarking of goods and merchandises without the knowledge of the *fiscal* or his deputy, are not observed as they ought to be, whereby the honorable company is subjected to serious loss of revenue, wherein, then, it is necessary to provide. Therefore, the director general and council of New Netherland hereby order that the above-mentioned ordinances and edicts be held in stricter observance, and, further that no man, of whatever condition he may be, shall attempt to load any goods or merchandises, however named, in any barges, boats, scows or other craft, in order to transport them on board of the return ships or any other vessels, before and until the same are duly recorded with the *fiscal* or his substitute, and a permit to load them be obtained, on pain of confiscation of such goods as shall be found shipped without a proper permit. Let everyone be warned hereby and take heed against loss.

Done at Fort Amsterdam in New Netherland, the 24th of August 1657.

[16^1:119]

[ORDINANCE REGULATING CURRENCY]

The director general and council of New Netherland, to all those who shall hear this read.

Let it be known that whereas, both by their own experience and by manifold complaints of inhabitants and strangers, they are sufficiently, to their sorrow, daily informed and importuned respecting the great,

---

* Also in *LO*, 314–15. In a letter dated December 29, 1657, the directors write Stuyvesant that they have approved his ordinance with some changes to be seen in the printed copies. See *NYCD*, 12:69; extract translated in *LO*, 315. See *LWA*, 63 for prior ordinance.

excessive and intolerable high prices of necessary commodities and household articles, arising, among other causes, principally from the high price, far beyond their value, of beaver and other peltries in this country, in consequence of the abundance of sewant, which has run up to 10, 11 and 12 guilders for one beaver. And sewant being still, for want of struck or stamped coin, the most general currency between man and man, and buyer and seller, the prices of household commodities and common daily necessaries range according to that rate, and are from time to time dearer, indeed, 30, 40, sometimes 50 percent difference is made not only by the merchants, factors and wholesale traders, but also, consequently, by the shopkeepers, tradespeople, brewers, bakers, tavernkeepers, grocers and others if they work and sell goods beaver or sewant. This then, creates considerable confusion on the one hand, and on the other, great burdens, loss and damage as well to the majority of the inhabitants as to the company and its servants, insomuch that, by reason of the aforesaid inordinate and excessive prices of necessaries, the superior and inferior magistrates of this province are blamed and accused both by strangers and residents; the country in general has received a bad name, some greedy people not hesitating to sell even the most necessary supplies, articles of food and drink, according to their insatiable covetousness, at intolerable prices for sewant, namely:

A quart of poor vinegar at 24 stivers,
oil at 3 to 4 guilders,
A can of French wine at 40 to 45 stivers,
Two quarts of home brewed beer 12 stivers,
A tun of small beer at 8 guilders,
A tun of strong beer at 24 guilders,
A pair of coarse Faroese stockings at 4 guilders,
A pair of shoes at 6 to 7 guilders,
and all other necessaries in proportion. Which high prices are generally excused on the grounds that 30, 40 to 50 percent is lost on the sewant before it can be traded off for beaver.

The aforesaid director general and council, wishing to provide and to introduce some better order herein, as far as possible, for the advantage of all in general and in particular, have not been able to discover, after much serious consideration and advice, even of the lords patroons themselves, any better expedient than to declare sewant in trade an absolute merchandise, to buy, barter, sell and rebarter it at wholesale, according to the value and quality thereof. But inasmuch as sewant, for want of gold and silver coin, as already stated, must still serve as smaller change for daily necessaries between man and man, buyer and seller, the director general and council have judged it necessary to reduce, at the general office, the sewant due the company for rents or other outstanding debts; and also, consequently, to keep, receive and pay it out at beaver value, the beaver being reckoned still, and until further notice from the fatherland, at 8 guilders. Therefore, fixing and reducing the sewant at the general office, provisionally, from six to eight white ones for one stiver, and from three to four black ones for one stiver, at which rate sewant shall be received and paid out, after the publication and posting hereof, at the general office, without any distinction of persons; provided that the wares, labor or services charged to the company shall be computed according to the value so much lower, at least not higher, than the price of beaver. If, on the other hand, the receivers are willing to continue the old rate, the director general and council resolve and ordain that the company, or its servants on its part, can then agree respecting the quantity of portion of sewant, as it is ordinarily current.

Further, in order to cause the least disturbance and loss among the inhabitants, who may have in their possession a large quantity of sewant, and as sewant is esteemed, in the matter of commerce, an absolute commodity, as already stated, the director general and council do not intend, by this reduction of the sewant at the general office, any alteration or impairing of any private contracts, agreements or sales of merchandise heretofore made or hereafter to be made between man and man, buyer and seller; but in order to prevent all exception and complaint that no notice or warning had been given, which may be set up or pretended by one debtor or another at the Company's office, the director general and council hereby give notice, that, although the payment at the company's office is made to the creditors in manner as aforesaid, according to this reduction, immediately after the publication hereof, the debtors to the company's office may pay six white and three black ones for one stiver, for the space of three consecutive months, but if they make no payment in that time, the director general and council give notice and ordain that after the expiration of three months, all payments which must be made at the company's office in sewant, shall be in conformity to this enacted ordinance.

Thus done and published at Fort Amsterdam in New Netherland, the 29th of November 1657.*

---

* See *LWA*, 76 for prior ordinance. Also in *LO*, 317–20.

[16^1:122]

[ORDINANCE ANNULLING FRAUDULENT SALES OF
MORTGAGED LANDS ON THE SOUTH RIVER]

NOTICE

Whereas the director general and council of New Netherland are informed and importuned by petitions of diverse merchants and inhabitants both of the city of Amsterdam and of the village of Beverwijck, that they had long since advanced to various inhabitants at the South River in New Netherland, residing at that time in the neighborhood of the former forts, Nassau and Casamier, diverse merchandise for the payment whereof the greater portion of the aforesaid inhabitants have hypothecated and pledged by mortgage their lands, houses, lots and other real estate, which lands, houses and lots (as the creditors have credibly informed the director general and council) the aforesaid debtors have, on the establishment of the colony of New Amstel, endeavored, to their creditors' wrong, to sell, alienate and to transport to one and another of the colony's aforesaid colonists, which is directly contrary to all laws, statutes and equity; such sale and conveyance made without the previous knowledge of the creditors and contrary to the executed mortgages are hereby declared null and void, and the purchasers are warned that they have not to pay the same without notice thereof be first made in due form, on pain of being obliged to pay it once again to the creditors on the older bond or mortgage, authorized thereto either preferentially or concurrently.

Thus done in the session of the director general and council held at Fort Amsterdam in New Netherland, the 15th of December 1657.*

[16^1:123]

[ORDINANCE RENEWING AND AMPLIFYING
FIRE SAFETY REGULATIONS]

The director general and council of New Netherland, to all those who see this or hear this read, greetings.

Let it be known that they, to prevent the calamity of fire, did long ago condemn thatched roofs and wooden and plastered chimneys within this city, and to that end appointed fire wardens and inspectors, which by-law

---

*   Also in *LO*, 321.

and ordinance, the aforesaid director general and council, have often published and renewed,* but, it has, hitherto, been carelessly or obstinately neglected by many inhabitants, because the fine or penalty affixed thereto is either entirely too small, or the penalty is not enforced as it ought to be; by which negligence now and again diverse calamities and accidents have been caused and are still to be apprehended from fire; indeed, a total ruin of this city, in as much as it daily begins to be compactly built, so that provision must absolutely be made therein; to which end, the aforesaid director general and council, have deemed it proper and necessary not only to renew their previously enacted by-law and edicts, but also to amplify the same, and to increase the penalty thereof and to put it promptly into execution.

Therefore, the director general and council do ordain, that all thatched roofs and wooden chimneys, hay barracks and haystacks within this city, shall be removed and taken away within the time of four consecutive months after the publication hereof, under a fine of 50 guilders to be forfeited every month, and to be promptly put in execution for every house whether small or large, hay barrack, hay stack or wooden chimney, hen houses and hog pens included, that may be found within the walls of this city at the expiration of the aforesaid four months; the fine to be applied one-third for the officer who shall levy execution; the two other third parts for the behoof of this city. If in the meanwhile any fire should break out in any such chimneys or houses, a quadruple fire penalty, namely, one hundred guilders to be applied according to the previously enacted edict.

Further, whereas in all well ordered cities and towns it is customary that fire buckets, ladders and hooks be found provided about the corners of streets and in public houses, in order to be the better prepared in time of need, which is more necessary here than elsewhere, because, for want of brick, many wooden houses are built within this city, the one adjoining the other; therefore, the director general and council order and authorize the burgomasters of this city, that they, of themselves, or by their treasurer, shall at once promptly demand, collect or cause to be collected, from each house, whether large or small, one beaver or eight guilders in sewant, according to the rate at the office, in order, with the proceeds thereof, to send, by the first opportunity, to the fatherland for one hundred to 150 leather fire buckets, and for the balance to have some fire ladders and fire hooks immediately made, and, further, once a year, from each chimney, one guilder for a supplement and repairs thereof.

* This ordinance was passed in 1648; see *LO*, 82.

Thus done in the session of the director general and council held at Fort Amsterdam in New Netherland, the 15th of December 1657.*

[16¹:125]

[ORDINANCE AGAINST BRAWLING IN NEW AMSTERDAM]

Whereas the director general and council of New Netherland observe daily to their sorrow, that their previously issued ordinance enacted on the subject of quarreling, fighting, beating and striking, is not according to their good intent and meaning complied with, observed and obeyed as it ought to be, but despised and violated for a mere word by some quarrelsome persons, because of the small fine imposed by the aforesaid ordinance, which is sufficiently manifest as some persons have not even hesitated to say in the officer's presence, "It is only a matter of a pound Flemish in sewant"; being desirous to provide herein, in order to hinder and prevent further mischiefs which usually follow such fights, therefore the aforesaid director general and council do hereby most expressly forbid any street brawls or quarrels, much less beating and striking one another, since these can excite only provocations, mischiefs, indeed, murders; on pain of paying by the transgressors and violators hereof, as a fine for a simple blow of a fist, twenty-five guilders, and in case blood shall follow, four times as much, and if such happen in the presence of the officer, burgomaster or *schepen*, a double fine, to be applied as that behooves. Let everyone be hereby warned and take heed of loss.

Amsterdam in New Netherland, the 15th of December 1657.†

[16¹:126]

[ORDINANCE FOR APPRAISING AND ASSESSING VACANT LOTS IN NEW AMSTERDAM]

The director general and council of New Netherland, seeing and observing by daily experience that the previous ordinance and edicts are not obeyed according to the true meaning thereof, but, notwithstanding the repeated renewal of them, that many spacious and large lots, even in the best and most convenient part of this city, lie and remain without

---

* Also in *LO*, 322.

† Also in *LO*, 324. Ordinances against drawing knives were enacted in 1642 and amplified in 1647 (LO, 33 and 62); however, they did not cover street brawling.

buildings and are kept by the owners either for greater profit, or for pleasure, and others are thereby prevented to build for the promotion of population and increase of trade and consumption, as well as for the embellishment of this city, whereunto many newcomers would be encouraged in case they could procure a lot at a reasonable price on a suitable location, agreeably to the foregoing edicts. Which neglect, if not contempt thereof, in reserving and retaining such extensive and spacious lots, whether for profit or for pleasure, is owing principally to the fact that no penalty or fine is imposed by the forementioned edicts, and that the proprietary owners are, for a great many years, occupying and reserving the lots free of any tax in expectation of greater profit, or using them for pleasure, as orchards and gardens, whereby building and population, and consequently the advancement of commerce, consumption and the prosperity of this city are retarded, contrary to the good intent and meaning of the directors of the Chartered West India Company, lords and patroons of this province, as first grantors and distributors of the lots with a view, to have the same built on for the embellishment, peopling, increase of the inhabitants, trade, consumption and prosperity of this city, as expressed in the granted patents, with the additional stipulation and submission: Of such taxes as may be imposed thereon by the aforesaid lords or their agents, In observance and obedience whereof the aforesaid director general and council have lately caused the vacant and unimproved lots to be measured by their sworn surveyor in the presence of the burgomasters of this city, according to the survey of the streets, and found some hundreds of lots inside the walls of this city vacant and not built on. In order that these may be the sooner built on, in accordance with the good intention and meaning of the aforesaid directors, agreeably to the previously enacted ordinances, indeed, that the disorder arising from the possession, free of any tax, of such spacious and extensive lots for profit or pleasure, may be prevented, and those who are inclined to build may be accommodated with lots at a reasonable price, the director general and council hereby ordain, in amplification of the above-mentioned edicts, that all vacant and unbuilt on lots which were lately measured and laid out by the surveyor of the director general and council, be immediately after the publication and posting hereof, assessed and appraised, first and foremost by the owners in possession, themselves, to the end that they may not hereafter complain of under valuation, and that so long as the owner retains the lot or lots, or allows them to remain without proper and habitable houses built thereon, he shall pay for the same yearly the 15th penny in two installments, the one half on May day; the proceeds to be applied to the fortification of this city and the repairs thereof.

And the burgomasters are authorized and ordered after the publication hereof, to summon the owners of the lots without regard of persons before them at the city hall of this city; to cause the assessment to be made; to have it recorded by their secretary in due form, and to have the proceeds received by their treasurer, and in case of opposition or refusal, to fine the obstinate person civilly; to appraise his lots according to the value and the situation of the locality, on condition that it be left to the choice of the owner in possession to retain the lots appraised by the burgomasters on payment, as stated, of the 15th penny thereof, or otherwise to give them up for that price to the burgomasters for the benefit of the city.

It remains in like manner, on the other hand, at the option of the aforesaid burgomasters to take the lots appraised by the owner himself, for the account of the city, and to convey them to others who are disposed and ready to build, at that price, if the owner himself will not, or cannot build in conformity to the aforesaid edicts, or to leave them to the owner until they are built on by themselves or others, when the impost or tax imposed for valid reasons on the unimproved lots, shall cease.

And in order to promote the population, settlement, beauty, strength and prosperity of this city, the director general and council ordain and command that, from this time forward, no dwelling houses shall be built near or under the walls or gates of this city, before or until the lots herein mentioned are properly built on.

Thus done in the session of director general and council held at Fort Amsterdam in New Netherland, the 15th of January 1658.*

[16^1:129]

[ORDINANCE REQUIRING PARTIES TO MARRY AFTER PUBLICATION OF THEIR BANNS]

Whereas the director general and council of New Netherland not only are informed, by have even seen and remarked, that some persons, after the proclamation and publication, for the third time, of their banns or intentions of marriage, do not proceed further with the solemnization of their marriage as they ought, but postpone it from time to time, not only

* Also in *LO*, 325–27.

weeks, but some months, which is directly contrary to, and in contravention of the good order and custom of our fatherland, wherein being
willing to provide, in order to prevent the mischiefs and irregularities
which will flow therefrom.

Therefore, the aforesaid director general and council do hereby ordain
that all published persons, after three proclamations have been made and
no lawful impediment occurs, shall cause their marriages to be solem-
nized within one month at furthest, after the last proclamation, or within
that time, appear and show cause where they ought, for refusing; and that
on pain of forfeiting ten guilders for the first week after the expiration
of the aforesaid month, and for the succeeding weeks 20 guilders for
each week, until they have made known the reasons for refusing.

Furthermore, no man and woman shall be at liberty to keep house as
married persons, before and until they are lawfully married, on pain of
forfeiting one hundred guilders, more or less, as shall be appropriate to
their situation and all such persons may be fined anew for it every month
by the officer, according to the order and custom of our fatherland.

Thus done at the session held at Fort Amsterdam in New Netherland, the
15th of January 1658.*

[16[1]:130]

[ORDINANCE REGULATING DUTIES AND FEES OF NOTARIES AND OTHER OFFICERS]

Whereas the director general and council of New Netherland are sufficiently convinced, as well by their own experience, even, by several bills
of costs, exhibited before them, as by the remonstrances and complaints
of others presented to them, of the exactions of secretaries, notaries,
clerks and other commissioned persons, in suing and prosecuting con-
tending parties; of the excessively great fees and charges for writing of
almost all sorts of instruments, to the serious, indeed nearly intolerable,
onerousness of the judgment and costs of court; some being so far seized
by avarice and greed that they are ashamed to tender a bill, or specification of the fee they demand, but ask, if not extort, the amount from parties
in gross; the aforesaid director general and council, being desirous to
provide therein for the better and more supportable promotion of justice,
do hereby ordain, enact and command that from this time forward, no

* Also in *LO*, 328–29.

man shall undertake to draw up or to write any public instrument, unless he be commissioned or licensed thereto by the director general and council, as secretary, notary or clerk, which commissioned or licensed person is bound to content himself with such fee as is established for it by the director general and council, and to renew every year, on the 5th of February, the oath which he has taken, precisely to submit to and obey the ordinance enacted, or hereafter, according to circumstances, to be enacted, on the subject of secretaries, notaries, clerks and such like officers, in conformity to the following:

First, all secretaries, notaries, clerks, or such officers, shall keep a correct register or journal, in which people may see immediately, if necessary and when required, whatever has been executed before them, and for which they demand such fee and place it on their account.

Secondly, no secretary, notary, clerk, or any such officer, shall demand from any person any money in advance, or ask or take any present, or be at liberty to compound or agree with anyone about a fee and pay for writing yet to be earned, inasmuch as such composition and previous agreement, before final judgment, must redound to the injury of the succumbing party, in case he be condemned in the expenses and costs of court; but the aforesaid officers may receive their pay according to this ordinance, either at any time before the execution of the instrument, or at the end of the suit, on rendering proper account and specification of what they have written, what errands they have done, what they have performed or copied, without entering any extraordinary costs in gross, in such account or specification, but all according to the fee allowed for it; not being permitted either to demand or to exact anything else or more from their clients, on pain of forfeiture of office and fifty guilders fine, by such as may be found to have acted contrary hereunto.

Thirdly, the secretary, notary, clerk or officer shall sign with his own hand all instruments executed in his presence, and seal them, when required, with his signet, providing that he receive for his seal six stivers in addition to the legal fee.

Fourthly, secretaries, notaries, clerks and such like officers shall be bound, when required, to give a discharge or receipt for the earned and paid fee, to be made use of when necessary.

Finally and lastly, all secretaries, notaries and clerks shall be bound to serve the poor and indigent, who ask such as an alms, *gratis* and *pro Deo*; and may demand and receive from the following fees:

For a simple petition written on one side of the paper, 18 stivers.

If the petitioner desire to have it recorded or registered;
for copying, 12 stivers.

For a simple summons, as above, 18 stivers.

For an answer, reply or rejoinder, 2 guilders.

For engrossing; for copying, 24 stivers.

But if the answer, reply rejoinder, summons or petition require more than one half sheet of paper, for each page of 25 to 30 lines, 30 to 36 letters in a line, 30 stivers.

For a deduction; each half sheet of 26 to 30 lines, 30 to 36 letters in the line, 2 guilders.

For a petition in appeal to be presented to the director general and council, 2 guilders 10 stivers.

For a petition of revision, review, purging, reduction, rehearing, complaint, pardon, or liberty to return to the country, to be presented to the director general and council, 2 guilders 10 stivers.

If it happens to exceed the second of third page (lines and letters as before), per page, 24 stivers.

For a petition of the same nature as above, to any inferior court, 36 to 40 stivers.

Or per page (lines and letters as before), 20 stivers.

For a judgment, 30 stivers.

For extracts from their books (lines and letters as before) per page, 20 stivers.

For a contract, obligation, assignment, attestation, lease, or bill of sale, 30 stivers.

For the copy, 20 stivers.

For a verbal consultation on a case depending before the director general and council, 20 stivers; but the notary is bound to enter in his journal the time and subject.

For an inventory of documents to be furnished by parties, 15 stivers.

For drawing up interrogatories and entering the questions, per half page, 10 stivers; provided that 7 to 8 interrogatories stand on one page. For the answer to be entered on the opposite side, in like manner, 10 stivers.

For one day's journey with or without their client, when required, exclusive of carriage hire and board, 4 guilders.

But within the city, village or place, accompanying their client, when required, 20 stivers.

For attending a term of court, with or without their client, 15 stivers; neglecting to attend it, to pay default and damages thereof.

No disbursements for drink, or any other extraordinary presents, gifts, or gratuities shall be brought into any account, or demanded or collected by the secretaries, notaries, clerks or such like officers.

And this and the foregoing articles shall not only be published, posted and observed in all places within this New Netherland province, where publication is usually made, but also read by the *fiscal*, *schout* and other inferior magistrates privately in their respective courts, before the secretaries, notaries, clerks and such like, now and on the 5th of February, not being Sunday, in every succeeding year, and thereupon the oath exacted from them to regulate themselves precisely in conformity thereto, and in case of refusal to be removed from their office and place, with express prohibition neither directly nor indirectly to write any instruments for any person under a penalty of 50 guilders for the first, twice as much for the second time, and an arbitrary correction at the discretion of the judge for the third offense.

Thus done at the session of the honorable director general and council of New Netherland held in Fort Amsterdam in New Netherland, the 25th of January 1658.*

[16^1:135]

[ORDINANCE ESTABLISHING A NEW VILLAGE AT THE NORTHERN END OF MANHATTAN ISLAND]†

The director general and council of New Netherland hereby give notice, that for the further promotion of agriculture, for the security of this island and the cattle pasturing thereon, as well as for the greater recreation and amusement of this city of Amsterdam, in New Netherland, they have resolved to form a new village or settlement at the end of the island, and near the lands of Jochem Pietersen, deceased, and those which adjoin thereto. In order that the lovers of agriculture may be encouraged thereto, the aforesaid proposed new village is favored by the director general and

---

*   Also in *LO*, 329–33.

†   This new village was originally named New Haerlem, and eventually became known as Harlem.

council with the following privileges:

First, each of the inhabitants thereof shall receive by lot, in full ownership 18, 20 to 24 morgens of arable land, 6 to 8 morgens of marshland, and be exempt from tenths for 15 years commencing next May, on condition that he pay within the course of three years, in installments, eight guilders for each morgen of tillage land for the behoof of the interested, or their creditors, who are now or formerly were driven from the aforesaid lands, and have suffered great loss thereon.

Secondly, in order to prevent similar damage from calamities or expulsions, the director general and council promise the inhabitants of the aforesaid village to protect and maintain them with all their power, and when notified and required, to assist them with 12 to 15 soldiers on the monthly pay of the company, the village providing quarters and rations; this whenever the inhabitants may petition for it.

Thirdly, when the aforesaid village has 20 to 25 families, the director general and council will favor it with an inferior court of justice; and, for that purpose, a double number is to be nominated out of the most discreet and proper persons, for the first time by the inhabitants and afterward by the magistrates thereof, and presented annually to the director general and council, to elect a single number therefrom.

Fourthly, the director general and council promise to employ all possible means that the inhabitants of the aforesaid village, when it has the above-mentioned number of families, will be accommodated with a good, pious orthodox minister, toward whose maintenance the director general and council promise to pay half the salary; the other half to be supplied by the inhabitants in the best and easiest manner, with the advice of the magistrates of the aforesaid village, at the most convenient time.

Fifthly, the director general and council will assist the inhabitants of the aforesaid village, whenever it will best suit their convenience, to construct, with company's Negroes, a good wagon road from this place to the village aforesaid, so that people can travel to and from it on horseback and with a wagon.

Sixthly, in order that the advancement of the aforesaid village may be the sooner and better promoted, the director general and council have resolved and determined not to establish, or allow to be established, any new villages or settlements before and until the aforesaid village be brought into existence; certainly not until the aforesaid number of inhabitants is completed.

Seventhly, for the better and greater promotion of neighborly correspondence with the English of the north, the director general and council will at a more convenient time, authorize a ferry and suitable scow near the aforesaid village, in order to convey cattle and horses, and favor the aforesaid village with a cattle and horse market.

Eighthly, whoever are inclined to settle themselves, or to have servants set up some farms there, shall be bound to enter their names at once or within a short time at the office of the secretary of the director general and council, and to begin immediately with others to place on the land one able-bodied person provided with proper arms, or in default thereof to be deprived of his right.

Thus done at the session of the director general and council held at Fort Amsterdam in New Netherland, the 4th of March 1658.*

* Also in *LO*, 335.

Writs of Appeal
1658–1663

New Netherland Documents Series
Volume XVI, part one

[16⁴:1]

[SAMUEL MAHU APPEALS A JUDGMENT
IN FAVOR OF NICOLAS BOOTH]

Petrus Stuyvesant, on behalf of their honorable High Mightinesses, the lords States general of the United Netherlands, and the honorable lords directors of the Chartered West India Company, chamber at Amsterdam, director general of N. Netherland, Curaçao, Bonaire, Aruba and dependencies thereof, together with the honorable lords councilors, have summoned hereto the court messenger, Claes van Elslant *de Jonge*, greetings.

Whereas Samuel Mahu has remonstrated to us by petition that he finds himself greatly injured by the judgment handed down by the honorable burgomasters and *schepenen* of this city dated 29 May, between him and Nicolaes Booth,* because Nicolaes Booth was permitted and allowed to collect 2460 pounds of tobacco in the Virginias (for which he is indebted to the aforesaid Mahu, as per balance), and then, at the risk of the aforesaid Mahu [he was allowed] not to freight it there until this coming October and bring it to this place, notwithstanding that the aforesaid Claes Booth himself confesses and admits to having already received the aforesaid tobacco. For this our assistance is requested.

Therefore, we order you to summon the aforesaid Nicolaes Booth to appear here before us in Fort Amsterdam next Tuesday, being the 9th of July,† or to send a deputy, to respond to any demands and rejoinders that the aforesaid Samuel Mahu shall make or effect against him, inviting those of the aforesaid court to appear or to send deputies on the day stated above (if it pleases them) in order to see us annul or confirm the aforesaid judgment; providing copies for use of the parties, and relating to us what you encounter.‡

[Last line(s) destroyed.]

---

* Mahu was suing Booth for delivery of tobacco in accordance with their contract. See *Records of New Amsterdam*, 2:394–95 (hereafter cited as *RNA*).

† The date of this document is most likely July 2, 1658.

‡ The council upheld the decision of the court of New Amsterdam and denied Mahu's appeal; see NYCM, 8:929.

[16⁴:2]

[JACOB VIS APPEALS A JUDGMENT IN FAVOR OF FREDERICK LUBBERTSEN]

Petrus Stuyvesandt, on behalf of their honorable High Mightinesses the lords States General of the United Netherlands and the lords directors of the Chartered West India Company, chamber of Amsterdam, director general of N. Netherland, Curaçao, Bonaire, Aruba and the dependencies thereof, together with the honorable lords councilors, have summoned hereto the court messenger, Claes van Elslant *de Jonge*, greetings.

Whereas Jacob Vis has demonstrated to us by petition that he finds himself greatly injured by the judgment handed down by the honorable court of this city dated the 17th of July, between him and Frederick Lubbertsen, because he was condemned by the aforesaid judgment, on pain of attachment, to pay *f*230 to Frederick Lubbertsen for the account of Jacob van Couwenhoven, because he was ordinary security for it, without having first attempted to attach the aforesaid Jacob van Couwenhoven as the principal debtor (so he says) according to legal form and custom. For this our assistance is requested.*

Therefore, we order you to summon the aforesaid Frederick Lubbertsen to appear here before us in Fort Amsterdam next Tuesday, being the 9th of July, or to send a deputy, to respond to any demands and rejoinders that the aforesaid Jacob Vis shall make or effect against him, notifying those of the aforesaid court to appear or to send deputies on the day stated above (if it pleases them) in order to see us annul or confirm the aforesaid judgment; providing copies for use of the parties, and relating to us what you encounter.†

Done at Fort Amsterdam the 2nd of July 1658,

(and was signed)
P. Stuyvesant.

* Jacob Vis was security for Jacob Wolfersen van Couwenhoven in the purchase of a horse from Lubbertsen. When Wolfersen defaulted on his payment, Vis was ordered to pay in his stead. See *RNA*, 2:172, 386, 388 and 400 for this case.
† On July 9th the council upheld Vis's appeal, see NYCM, 8:908.

[16⁴:3]

[WILLEM DOUKLES APPEALS A JUDGMENT IN FAVOR OF
JAN HENDRICKS *GLAESEMAECKER*]

Petrus Stuyvesant, on behalf of their honorable High Mightinesses, the lords States General of the United Netherlands, and the honorable lords directors of the chartered West India Company, chamber at Amsterdam, director general of N. Netherland, Curaçao, Bonaire, Aruba and dependencies thereof, together with the honorable lords councilors, have summoned hereto the court messenger, Claes van Elslant *de Jonge*, greetings.

Whereas Willem Doukles has remonstrated to us by petition that he finds himself greatly injured by the judgment handed down by the burgomasters and *schepenen* of this city dated 15 June last past, between him and Jan Hendricks *Glaesemaecker*,* because he was condemned by the aforesaid judgment to pay the plaintiff, Jan Hendricx, notwithstanding he requested a copy of the demand in order to respond to it in writing on the next court day. This was denied him therefore he has not answered in his defense (so he says). For this our assistance is requested.†

Therefore, we order you to summon the aforesaid Jan Hendricx to appear here before us in Fort Amsterdam next Tuesday, being the 9th of July, or to send a deputy, to respond to any demands and rejoinders that the aforesaid Willem Doukles shall make or effect against him inviting those of the aforesaid court to appear or to send deputies on the date stated above (if it please them) in order to see us annul or confirm the aforesaid judgment; providing copies for use of the parties, and relating to us what you encounter.

Done at Fort Amsterdam in N. Netherland the 2nd of July 1658, (and was signed) P. Stuyvesant

[16⁴:4]

[JACOB JANSEN HUYS APPEALS A JUDGMENT
IN FAVOR OF ALLARD ANTHONY]

Petrus Stuyvesant, on behalf of their honorable High Mightinesses, the lords States General of the United Netherlands, and the honorable lords

---

* glazier
† See *RNA*, 2:403 for this judgment. The council reversed the court's decision on July 9th. See NYCM, 8:907.

directors of the chartered West India Company, chamber at Amsterdam, director general of N. Netherland, Curaçao, Bonaire, Aruba and dependencies thereof, together with the honorable lords councilors, have summoned hereto the court messenger, Pieter Schaeffbanck, greetings.

Whereas Mattheus de Vos, in the capacity of proxy for Jacob Jansen Huys, former skipper on the ship *De Peereboom,** has demonstrated to us by petition that he finds himself gravely injured, in the aforesaid capacity, for reasons shown to us in the judgment handed down by the honorable burgomasters and *schepenen* of this city dated 7 January, last past, between Jacob Jansen Huys and *Sr*. Allard Anthony. For this our assistance is requested.†

Therefore, we order you to summon the aforesaid Allard Anthony to appear here before us in Fort Amsterdam on Thursday, being the 29th of this month, or to send a deputy, to respond to any demands and rejoinders that the aforesaid Mattheus de Vos shall make or effect against him, inviting those of the aforesaid court to appear or to send deputies on the date stated above (if it please them) in order to see us annul or confirm the aforesaid judgment; providing copies for use of the parties, and relating to us what you encounter.

The 15th of August 1658, (and was signed) P. Stuyvesant

[16⁴:5]

[ANTONY CLAESEN MOORE APPEALS A JUDGMENT IN FAVOR OF MATTHEUS DE VOS]

Petrus Stuyvesant, on behalf of their honorable High Mightinesses, the lords States General of the United Netherlands, and the honorable lords directors of the chartered West India Company, chamber at Amsterdam, director general of N. Netherland, Curaçao, Bonaire, Aruba and dependencies thereof, together with the honorable lords councilors, have summoned hereto the court messenger, Pieter Schaeffbanck, greetings.

Whereas Antony Claesen Moore has remonstrated to us by petition that he finds himself greatly injured for reasons shown to us in the judgment handed down by the honorable court of this city dated 17 September, last

---

*   the Peartree

†   The court's decision was based on a six-part award of the arbitrators; see *RNA*, 2:292–93.

past, between him and Mattheus de Vos. For this our assistance is requested.*

Therefore, we order you to summon the aforesaid Mattheus de Vos to appear here before us in Fort Amsterdam on Thursday, being the 17th of this month, or to send a deputy, to respond to any demands and rejoinders that he aforesaid Antony Claesen Moore shall make or effect against him, inviting those of the aforesaid court to appear or to send deputies on the date stated above (if it please them) in order to see us annul or confirm the aforesaid judgment; providing copies for use of the parties, and relating to us what you encounter.

Done in Fort Amsterdam in N. Netherland on the 9th of October 1658.†

[16⁴:6]

[JOHN ARTCHER APPEALS JUDGMENT IN FAVOR OF RICHARD PANTON.

Petrus Stuyvesant, on behalf of their honorable High Mightinesses, the lords States General of the United Netherlands, and the honorable lords directors of the chartered West India Company, chamber at Amsterdam, director general of N. Netherland, Curacao, Bonaire, Aruba and dependencies thereof, together with the honorable lords councilors, have summoned hereto the court messenger, Claes van Elslant *de Jong*, greetings.

Whereas Jan Artcher, alias Jan Coopall, has remonstrated to us by petition that he finds himself greatly injured for reasons shown to us in the judgment handed down by the honorable court of Oostdurp dated 17 December, last past, between him and Richard Pantom, because he was condemned by the aforesaid judgment to pay Richard Pantom a sum of money, notwithstanding that he has demonstrated and proven that the aforesaid money is due to him from Richard Pantom (so he says). For this our assistance is requested.‡

Therefore, we order you to summon the aforesaid Richard Pantom to appear here before us in Fort Amsterdam on Thursday, being the 6th of February, or to send a deputy, to respond to any demands and rejoinders that the aforesaid Jan Artcher shall make or effect against him, inviting

---

* The court required Moore to pay a debt. See *RNA*, 3:10–11.

† The council upheld the court's decision on December 19th; see NYCM, 8:1071.

‡ See *Minutes of the Court of Sessions (1657–1696), Westchester County*, Dixon Ryan Fox, ed. (White Plains, N.Y., 1924) p. 4, for the Oostdurp court judgment.

who were the parties?

those of the aforesaid court to appear or to send deputies on the date stated above (if it please them) in order to see us annul or confirm the aforesaid judgment; providing copies for use of the parties, and relating to us what you encounter.

Done at our meeting held in Fort Amsterdam in New Netherland, the 23rd of January 1659.*

[16⁴:7]

[RITCHERT BRITNEL APPEALS A JUDGMENT IN FAVOR OF TOMAS IRELANDT AND DANIEL WHITHEAD]

Petrus Stuyvesant, on behalf of their honorable High Mightinesses, the lords States General of the United Netherlands, and the honorable lords directors of the chartered West India Company, chamber at Amsterdam, director general of N.Netherland, Curaçao, Bonaire, Aruba and dependencies thereof, together with the honorable lords councilors, have summoned hereto the court messenger, Claes van Elslant *de Jonge*, greetings.

Whereas Ritchert Britnel has remonstrated to us by petition that he finds himself greatly injured for reasons shown to us in the judgment handed down by the magistrates of Heemsteede dated the 2 and 16 January between him, and Tomas Irelandt and Daniel Whithead. For this our assistance is requested.

Therefore, we order you to summon the aforesaid Tomas Irelandt and Daniel Whithead to appear here before us in Fort Amsterdam on Thursday, being the 20th of March, or to send a deputy, to respond to any demands and rejoinders that the aforesaid Ritchert Britnel shall make or effect against them, inviting those of the aforesaid court to appear or to send deputies on the date stated above (if it please them) in order to see us annul or confirm the aforesaid judgment; providing copies for use of the parties, and relating to us what you encounter.

Done at our meeting held in Fort Amsterdam in N. Netherland, the 20th of February 1659.

Unpaid.

---

*   Council minutes for 1659 are missing, so the judgment on this case is not known; but according to Writ 11 on page 113, the judgment was apparently for Artcher.

[16⁴:8]

[ALLARD ANTHONY APPEALS JUDGMENT IN FAVOR OF
JACOB VAN COUWENHOVEN]

Petrus Stuyvesant, on behalf of their honorable High Mightinesses, the
lords States General of the United Netherlands, and the honorable lords
directors of the chartered West India Company, chamber at Amsterdam,
director general of N. Netherland, Curaçao, Bonaire, Aruba and dependencies thereof, together with the honorable lords councilors, have summoned hereto the court messenger, Claes van Elslant *de Jonge*, greetings.

Whereas Allard Anthony has remonstrated to us by petition that he finds
himself greatly injured by the judgment handed down by the honorable
court of this city, dated the end of January, last past, between him and
Jacob van Couwenhoven, because he was condemned to pay 10 guilders
for every pipe of rebrewed beer, whereas it is still the case that 10 guilders
be paid for every pipe of rebrewed Holland beer on the condition that
two are made from one etc. (so he says). For this our assistance is
requested.*

Therefore, we order you to summon the aforesaid Jacob van Couwenhoven to appear here before us in Fort Amsterdam on Thursday being
the 27th of February, or to send a deputy, to respond to any demands and
rejoinders that the aforesaid Allard Antony shall make or effect against
him, inviting those of the aforesaid court to appear or to send deputies
on the date stated above (if it please them) in order to see us annul or
confirm the aforesaid judgment; providing copies for use of the parties,
and relating to us what you encounter.

Done at our meeting held in Fort Amsterdam in N. Netherland, the 20th
of February 1659.

[16⁴:9]

[WARNAER WESSELS APPEALS A JUDGMENT
IN FAVOR OF JACOB BARSIMSON]

Petrus Stuyvesant, on behalf of their honorable High Mightinesses, the
lords States General of the United Netherlands, and the honorable lords
directors of the chartered West India Company, chamber at Amsterdam,

---

* The court's judgment is unknown because the *RNA* minutes from 27 September
1658 to 19 August 1659 are not among the records.

director general of N. Netherland, Curaçao, Bonaire, Aruba and dependencies thereof, together with the honorable lords councilors, have summoned hereto the court messenger, Claes van Elslant *de Jonge*, greetings.

Whereas Warnaer Wessels has remonstrated to us by petition that he finds himself greatly injured for reasons shown to us in the judgment handed down by the honorable court of this city, dated 29 January, last past, between him and Jacob Barsimson, Jew, because he was condemned to pay to the aforesaid Barsimson one hogshead of tobacco and some loose baskets, amounting to the quantity of 400 lb. at 7 stivers a pound that the aforesaid Barsimson claims to have left in the cellar of Warnaer Wessels, which the aforesaid Barsimson has not and cannot prove by all his submitted documents and declarations, so he says. For this our assistance is requested.*

Therefore, we order you to summon the aforesaid Jacob Barsimson to appear here before us in Fort Amsterdam on Thursday, being the 20th of March, or to send a deputy, to respond to any demands and rejoinders that the aforesaid Warnaer Wessels shall make or effect against him, inviting those of the aforesaid court to appear or to send deputies on the date stated above (if it please them) in order to see us annul or confirm the aforesaid judgment; providing copies for use of the parties, and relating to us what you encounter.

Done at our meeting held in Fort Amsterdam in N. Netherland, the 27th of February 1659.

[16⁴:10]

[ALLARD ANTHONY APPEALS A JUDGMENT IN FAVOR OF ANTHONY CLAESEN DE MOORE]

Petrus Stuyvesant, on behalf of their honorable High Mightinesses, the lords States General of the United Netherlands, and the honorable lords directors of the chartered West India Company, chamber at Amsterdam, director general of N. Netherland, Curaçao, Bonaire, Aruba and dependencies thereof, together with the honorable lords councilors, have summoned hereto the court messenger, Claes van Elslant *de Jonge*.

Whereas Allard Anthony has remonstrated to us by petition that he finds himself greatly injured for reason shown to us in the judgment handed

---

* Ibid.

down by the honorable court of this city, dated 18 February, between him and Anthony Claesen de Moore, because his just claim against the aforesaid de Moore for the sum of 183 pounds Flemish and 2 stivers, done by virtue of a certain disputed bill of exchange, was rejected by the aforesaid honorable court (so he demonstrates). For this our assistance is requested.*

Therefore, we order you to summon the aforesaid Anthony Claesen de Moore to appear here before us in Fort Amsterdam on Thursday, being the 20th of this month, or to send a deputy, to respond to any demands and rejoinders that the aforesaid Allard Anthony shall make or effect against him, inviting those of the aforesaid court to appear or to send deputies on the date stated above (if it please them) in order to see us annul or confirm the aforesaid judgment; providing copies for use of the parties, and relating to us what you encounter.

Done at our meeting held in Fort Amsterdam in N. Netherland, the 19th of March 1659, (was signed) P. Stuyvesant.

[16⁴:11]

[ORDER PUTTING JOHN ARTCHER IN POSSESSION OF GOODS BELONGING TO RICHARD PANTOM]

Whereas Jan Artcher has remonstrated and informed us that he requested satisfaction from Richard Pamton [sic] according to a judgment dated the 20th of this month, and as a result had some goods attached at Oostdurp, which attached goods were sold by the aforesaid Pantom, in contempt of justice, after the attachment was imposed and conveyed to others. He informed the magistrates of Oostdurp of this and requested their help and assistance in the matter, but was unable to receive any help or assistance (so he says). For this our assistance is requested.

Therefore, we have commissioned and ordered our provost marshal, Resolveert Waldron, and court messenger, Claes van Elslant to notify, charge and command the aforesaid magistrates that they should assist the aforesaid John Artcher as much as possible so that he may enjoy the effect of our aforesaid judgment, on pain of proceedings being instituted against them, as is appropriate, if they be found negligent herein; in addition, ordering the aforesaid persons, with the assistance of the aforesaid magistrates, to attach and impound the goods formerly belong-

* Ibid.

ing to the aforesaid Artcher and sold at the request of Pantom, together with as many of Pantom's goods as shall be necessary for satisfaction of the contents of the aforesaid judgment. In so doing justice shall be maintained and our earnest intention be carried out.*

Issued and done in Fort Amsterdam in N. Netherland, the 29th of March 1659, and affixed with the country's seal.

Note: Because this is an order
of the council, this warrant
was not paid for by the council.

[16⁴:12]

[SUMMONS TO PETER LE FEBER TO PAY ON A MORTGAGE]

Petrus Stuyvesant, on behalf of their honorable High Mightinesses, the lords States General of the United Netherlands, and the honorable lords directors of the chartered West India Company, chamber at Amsterdam, director general of N. Netherland, Curaçao, Bonaire, Aruba and dependencies thereof, together with the honorable lords councilors, have summoned hereto the count messenger, Pieter Schaeffbanck, greetings.

Whereas s[   ] Wallewijn vander Veen,† in his capacity as attorney for Cornelis Schut, has remonstrated to us by petition how the deceased Mr. Isaac Allerton ceded to him, the petitioner, his, Allerton's mortgage and rights to the farm of Pieter le Feber located on Long Island in the *Walebocht*‡ (secured for the sum of eleven hundred and twenty-nine guilders and 7 stivers in capital), as appears in the documents exhibited to us; and whereas the payments stated in the aforesaid documents have expired and no payment has been received, and whereas the farm is unoccupied and the oxen attached thereto (and also bound in the aforesaid mortgage) have been running in the woods without any supervision (so he says). For this our assistance is requested.

Therefore, we order you to inform the aforesaid Pieter le Feber that he has to pay the aforesaid sum to Waelewijn vander Veen within the period of 14 days after this date, on pain of having the requested attachment authorized, as is appropriate

---

* See *LWA*, 109 regarding this case.
† Vander Veen was a notary in New Amsterdam.
‡ Literally Walloon Bay, now Wallebout Bay of Long Island in the East River.

This done and issued under our hand and seal in Fort Amsterdam in N. Netherland, the 23rd [   ] 1659.*

[16⁴:13]

[JACOB VIS APPEALS A JUDGMENT IN FAVOR OF ANDRIES DE HAES]

Warrant with a writ of inhibition†

Petrus Stuyvesandt, on behalf of their honorable High Mightinesses the lords States General of the United Netherlands and the lords directors of the Chartered West India Company, chamber of Amsterdam, director-general of N. Netherland, Curaçao, Bonaire, Aruba and the dependencies thereof, together with the honorable lords councilors, have summoned hereto the court messenger, Claes van Elslant *de Jonge*.

Whereas Jacob Vis has remonstrated to us by petition that he finds himself greatly injured by a judgment handed down by the honorable court of this city, dated 28 October, between him and Andries de Haes, because the aforesaid judgment has ordered him to carry out the determination of certain mediators,‡ notwithstanding he offered to show proof of the mistakes made in the aforesaid determination (so he says). For this our assistance is requested.

Therefore, we order you to summon the aforesaid Andries de Haes to appear here before us in Fort Amsterdam on the first day of court or to send a deputy to respond to any demands and rejoinders that the aforesaid Jacob Vis shall make or effect against him, inviting those of the aforesaid court to appear (if it pleases them) on the aforementioned day, or to send deputies, in order to see us annul or confirm the aforesaid judgment. Furthermore, we order the aforesaid defendant and invited witnesses not to undertake or introduce anything prejudicial to the aforesaid appeal, but on the contrary, if anything were undertaken or introduced, then to return it immediately to its original state; providing copies for use of the

* The council's decision is unknown because the council minutes for 1659 are not among the records.

† An order from a superior court prohibiting an inferior court from further action in a case.

‡ Jacob Backer and Johannes de Peister were appointed arbitrators on September 6, 1659. They awarded to De Haes, who sued Vis for payment according to the award. Vis then asked the court for a revision to the award, which was denied. See *RNA*, 3:54 and 66.

parties, and relating to us what you encounter.

Done at our meeting held in Fort Amsterdam in N. Netherland, the 26th of November 1659.

Paid.

[16⁴:14]

[PIETER RUDOLPHUS APPEALS A JUDGMENT IN FAVOR OF BALTHAZAER D'HAERT]

Petrus Stuyvesandt, on behalf of their honorable High Mightinesses the lords States General of the United Netherlands and the lords directors of the Chartered West India Company, chamber of Amsterdam, director-general of N. Netherland, Curaçao, Bonaire, Aruba and the dependencies thereof, together with the honorable lords councilors, have summoned hereto the court messenger, Claes van Elslant *de Jonge*.

Whereas Pieter Rudolphus has remonstrated to us by petition that he finds himself greatly injured by the judgment handed down by the honorable court of this city dated 31 January, last past, between him and Balthazaer d'Haert, because he was condemned by the aforesaid judgment to satisfy and pay for the eight hogsheads of vinegar in question, according to sale, notwithstanding it was not true wine vinegar he bought (so he says). For this our assistance is requested.*

Therefore, we order you to summon the aforesaid Balthazaar d'Haert to appear here before us in Fort Amsterdam on Thursday, being the 18th of this month, or to send a deputy, to respond to any demands and rejoinders that the aforesaid Pieter Rudolphus shall make or effect against him, inviting those of the aforesaid court to appear or to send deputies on the day stated above (if it pleases them) in order to see us annul or confirm the aforesaid judgment; providing copies for use of the parties, and relating to us what you encounter.

Issued at our meeting held in Fort Amsterdam in N. Netherland, the 12th of April 1660, (was signed).

---

* See *RNA*, 3:120–21 for this case. The council confirmed the court of New Amsterdam's judgment. See NYCM, 9:273.

[16⁴:15]

[CORNELIS VAN GEZEL, CATARINA RAM AND PIETER
ALRICHS PUT IN POSSESSION OF JACOB ALRICHS'S
ESTATE UNDER BENEFIT OF INVENTORY]*

Petrus Stuyvesant, on behalf of the high and mighty lords States General
of the United Netherlands and the honorable lords directors of the
Chartered West India Company, director general of N. Netherland,
Curaçao, Bonaire, Aruba and dependencies thereof, together with the
lords councilors, greetings to all who see this or hear it read.

Let it be known that we have received the humble petition of Cornelis
van Gezel, Anna Catarina Ram and Pieter Alrichs, stating how their
uncle Jacob Alrichs, former director of the colony of New Amstel on the
South River of this world, died there, leaving behind possessions assigned to the petitioners according to testament.† Apprehensive that the
estate of their deceased uncle might be a burden with many debts or
claims so that the mere acceptance of it might be detrimental to the
petitioners, they deemed it inadvisable to accept the inheritance, other
than by benefit of inventory (so they say). For this reason they humbly
request to be granted an open letter from us which will serve this purpose.

Therefore, having taken the aforesaid matter into consideration, we have
given the petitioners leave and permission, as we give leave and permission by this our letter, that they, the petitioners, shall under benefit of
inventory be allowed to install themselves as heirs in the aforesaid house
of the deceased Jacob Alrichs, their uncle, and in this capacity take
possession and acceptance of the aforesaid house of the deceased together with the chattels, securities, debts and credits left behind by the
aforesaid Jacob Alrichs, provided that one of the appropriate officers of
the region, where most of the deceased's possessions are located, be
called in to make a good and honest inventory, with the express condition
that the petitioners shall be obligated to pledge good and sufficient
security from which to pay all the debts, bequests and legacies of the
aforesaid deceased, as much as the aforesaid possessions may cover,
without the petitioners being obligated to pay for any of the amount in
excess thereof; unless there still be a relative who has simply installed

* See appendix for additional papers related to this case.
† Jacob Alrichs died December 30, 1659. See *NYHM, Delaware Papers*, 18:184.
The colony of New Amstel was under the administration of the mayors of
Amsterdam from 1657 to 1664. Its jurisdiction eventually included the entire South
River region of New Netherland along the Delaware River, with an administrative
center at New Amstel (formerly Fort Casimir) now the city of New Castle, Delaware.

himself or intends to install himself as heir, then summon and order the officer of the place where the house of the deceased is located, and, in addition, all other magistrates and officers, each one as far as it may concern him, that the aforesaid inventory be honestly completed, and the security posted by the petitioners, and received and registered by the secretary here or in the colony of New Amstel; making sure that the petitioners are delivered of all assignable and inheritable possessions left behind by the aforesaid Jacob Alrichs, and allowing them to enjoy and use in peace and freedom the contents of this our present letter of benefit of inventory in the aforesaid manner and under the aforesaid limitations and modifications, without causing them any impediments or trouble; on the contrary, we hereby summon, command and commission our sergeant in the South River (hereto requested by the aforesaid petitioners and appellants of this our open letter) to go to the persons or residences of all creditors of the aforesaid house of the deceased, in addition to beneficiaries residing within this province, and to summon them on behalf of the high authorities of this province to appear, or to send deputies, before the court of the colony of New Amstel, where the house of the deceased is located, in order to see, there or wherever necessary, all the possessions left behind by the aforesaid deceased property inventoried and to see them appraised according to the ordinance* and the contents of this, and to post security by the aforesaid petitioners as is appropriate. In addition, we hereby authorize and commission him to summon all the same creditors and legatees, and all others who shall intend to oppose them, to appear, or to send deputies, before the court of the aforesaid colony in order to see them confirm the aforesaid letter of benefit of inventory with an explanation to them, with notification if they appear or send deputies; if not then proceedings shall still be instituted by the aforesaid court both for confirmation of the aforesaid letter of benefit of inventory, as otherwise according to the law. He is to relate his encounters with those of the aforesaid court whom we hereby expressly recommend (having heard the parties) to execute justice in a swift and equitable manner.

Thus done and issued in Fort Amsterdam in N. Netherland, the 25th of February 1660.

---

* For this ordinance see *LO*, 281.

[16⁴:15 (*bis*)]

[ABRAHAM VERPLANCKEN APPEALS A JUDGMENT
IN FAVOR OF RACHEL VINGE]

Petrus Stuyvesandt, on behalf of their honorable High Mightinesses the lords States General of the United Netherlands and the lords directors of the Chartered West India Company, chamber of Amsterdam, director-general of N. Netherland, Curaçao, Bonaire, Aruba and the dependencies thereof, together with the honorable lords councilors, have summoned hereto the court messenger, Claes van Elslant *de Jonge*, greetings.

Whereas Abraham Verplancken, husband and guardian of Maria Vinge, daughter of the deceased Adriane Cuvilje, for himself as well as for the other interested heirs, has remonstrated to us by petition that he finds himself greatly injured by the judgment handed down by the honorable court of this city, dated 26 January, last past, between him and Rachel Vinge because they, the defendants, were condemned to pay to the plaintiffs the sum of ƒ2041,14 in reference to a signed agreement dated 2 June 1655, and an increased sum and further account dated 2 October 1656, without taking into consideration a certain document of the defendants in which is shown that the defendants were not obligated by their signatures because of deceit by Tienhoven about which they have protested sufficiently against him and also taking into account the manifold and notable errors committed by Tienhoven to the disadvantage of the defendants as appears by the documents in the proceedings (so he says). For this our assistance is requested.

Therefore, we order you to summon the aforesaid Rachel Vinge* to appear before us here in Fort Amsterdam on Thursday, the 18th of this month, or to send a deputy to respond to any demands and rejoinders that the aforesaid Abraham Verplancken shall make or effect against her, inviting those of the aforesaid court to appear (if it pleases them) on the aforementioned day, or to send deputies to see us annul or confirm the aforesaid judgment; providing copies for use of the parties, and relating to us what you encounter. Done at our meeting held in Fort Amsterdam in N. Netherland, the 12th of April [   ].†

---

* Rachel Vinge was the wife of Cornelis van Tienhoven, former *fiscal* of the colony who disappeared in June of 1656; Maria Vinge was her sister; see, *RNA*, 2:349. The accounts do not appear in *RNA*.

† On August 12th the appeal was withdrawn in favor of Rachel van Tienhoven; see NYCM, 9:358.

[16⁴:16]

[JAN GERRITSEN VAN MARCKEN APPEALS A SENTENCE OF
BANISHMENT PRONOUNCED AT NEW AMSTEL]

Petrus Stuyvesandt, on behalf of their honorable High Mightinesses the
lords States General of the United Netherlands and the lords directors of
the Chartered West India Company, chamber of Amsterdam, director-
general of N. Netherland, Curaçao, Bonaire, Aruba and the dependencies
thereof, together with the honorable lords councilors, have summoned
hereto the sergeant, Jacob vander Veer, greetings.

Whereas Jan Gerritsen van Marcken, citizen of this city of Amsterdam
in N. Netherland, has shown us how he, petitioner, having been in the
South River at New Amstel in order to take care of his business there,
was at the house of a Master Evert Pietersen.* When the *schout* Gerrit
van Sweeringen came to fetch him, Evert, he, petitioner, said no more
than, "I would much rather go with soldiers than with the *schout*," the
same Gerrit van Sweeringen, and the president and councilor of New
Amstel, Alexander d'Hinojossa† and Jan Crato took such extreme and
injurious offense at it, letting malice push them so far that they not only
took their own depositions (appearing before special and unqualified
persons), but also took them from others as complaints against the
petitioner accusing him (but falsely) of mutiny, riot, slander etc., whereupon the aforesaid president, council, *schout* and other deponents (there
being not a single impartial person present in their sessions in the
capacity of judges and magistrates) on the 13th of February and the 6th
of March last past (after having imprisoned him several times, indeed,
threatened him with torture) resolved to banish the petitioner from N.
Amstel and send him to Holland; and furthermore fine him ƒ417,18,
which he also had to pay through Hendrick Kip; and even if the petitioner
protested against their incompetence and partiality before the director
general and council of N. Netherland, it would still not have helped, but
rather he had to do and say everything that they wished in order simply
to be released from them. Whereas he, petitioner, consequently finds
himself greatly offended and injured in this matter, and to have been
done an injustice (so he says), he therefore requests our assistance.

Therefore, we hereby order and commission you, Jacob vander Veer, at
the request of the aforesaid Jan Gerritsen van Marcken, to summon the

---

*   Evert Pietersen was employed as a school teacher by New Amstel.

†   Alexander d'Hinojossa became director of the city of Amsterdam's colony of
New Amstel upon the death Jacob Alrichs in 1659.

aforementioned president Alexander d'Hinojossa, the *schout* Gerrit van Sweeringen, and his councilors mentioned in the judgment and all others whom they might want to have come in this party, to appear or to send deputies before us here in Fort Amsterdam in New Netherland within the period of three weeks after the announcement of this in order to see the aforesaid judgment and its contents sustained and justified or, if they so deem it, to hear it disclaimed as null, void and invalid, adjusting and correcting it according to law, if such is appropriate, [and in order] to reply to such demands that the petitioner shall make at that time, so that, after the parties have been heard, we can furnish them with such a restitution of justice, and also of mercy, if necessary, as shall be found to be proper; furthermore forbidding and commending most vigorously in our name, upon severe penalty, the aforesaid defendants and all others, if required, that [   ] they not do, undertake nor [innovate] in prejudice of the aforesaid, nor of the aforesaid appellant Jan Gerritsen van Marcken which we with reason have raised against the needless interjection, exclamation and prosecution of his appeal; however, if something were done, undertaken, or innovated to the contrary, that they immediately and without delay repair the same and put it in its original and proper state, without being in any way remiss, and in case any of the aforesaid persons should move or absent themselves outside this province and precinct, then you shall make your announcement at their last place of residence; also, to their directors, deputies, and representatives of their possessions, if there be any one under our government who is not in New Amstel or in the most extreme place of this country (where such a summons is acceptable) and places located next to their residences, summoning them with your letter and authentic copy of this so that they cannot plead ignorance of it. When this announcement is made by you we shall consider it as valid as if it had been made to their persons, furnishing a copy of this and your announcement for the benefit of the defendants, and relating to us what you have done on the aforesaid day.

Issued in Fort Amsterdam in New Netherland under our distinctive seal and the signature of our secretary on the 12th of April 1660.*

---

* There are no further references to this case in the records.

[16⁴:17]

[INJUNCTION AGAINST ALEXANDER D'HINOJOSSA NOT TO MOLEST CORNELIS VAN GEZEL, AND TO TURN OVER JACOB ALRICHS'S PAPERS AND OTHER EFFECTS]

Petrus Stuyvesandt, on behalf of their honorable High Mightinesses the lords States General of the United Netherlands and the lords directors of the Chartered West India Company, chamber of Amsterdam, director general of N. Netherland, Curaçao, Bonaire, Aruba and the dependencies thereof, together with the honorable lords councilors, have summoned hereto the sergeant, Jacob vander Veer, greetings.

Let it be known that we have received the petition of Cornelis van Gezel, as executor of the testament of the late Mr. Jacob Alrichs, in his lifetime director in the colony of New Amstel, containing in effect how Alexander d'Hinojossa, contrary to the letters of benefit of inventory, and after our orders and instructions to him, continues to withhold the books and papers belonging to the estate; moreover, threatening to send him away with a bark if he bothers him with it anymore. Also, that he, d'Hinojossa, still has in his possession many effects belonging to the estate as well as some pertaining to his own defense, without being willing to hand over to him or the heirs any accounting or inventory; all in contempt of the letters of benefit and specific orders issued by us, so that he still remains disturbed in the peaceable administration of the estate, and powerless to advance matters of the same, tending to great damage and loss of the estate, and also to the defamation of the late Mr. Alrichs (so he says). He requests that he be supported in his administration and preservation of the aforesaid estate, and that he, d'Hinojossa, be ordered to hand over to him, petitioner, all effects and goods, together with papers, books, accounts, letters and copies of letters related to or concerned with the justification of the aforesaid estate, and that [   ] under proper inventory confirmed by oath [   ] noted.*

Therefore, we instruct and order hereby commissioning you thereto, that you address yourself to the person or to the residence of the aforesaid d'Hinojossa, and on our behalf command and order the same to leave the aforesaid petitioner unmolested in his administration; and furthermore to hand over to him under proper inventory, papers, books, accounts, letters and copies of letters related to the aforesaid estate and

---

* The problems between d'Hinojossa and Van Gezel are related in Willem Beeckman's letters to Petrus Stuyvesant in the *NYHM, Delaware Papers*, 18:184–89, 198, 237–38, 244. See also the appendix for papers related to this case.

might pertain to its settlement; in case of refusal or opposition, summon the defendant to come, or to send a deputy, on a certain, suitable day before us here at Manhattan in Fort Amsterdam, in order to relate the reasons thereof and to hear such demands and rejoinders that the petitioner shall make and effect against him, to respond to everything, and to proceed according to law. [In addition to] making copies, you are to relate to us what you encounter.

Done in Fort Amsterdam in N. Netherland under our distinctive seal and the signature of our secretary on the 19th of October 1660.

[16^4:18]

[CORNELIS VAN GEZEL APPEALS A JUDGMENT FROM THE COURT OF NEW AMSTEL]

Petrus Stuyvesandt, on behalf of their honorable High Mightinesses the lords States General of the United Netherlands and the lords directors of the Chartered West India Company, chamber of Amsterdam, director-general of N. Netherland, Curaçao, Bonaire, Aruba and the dependencies thereof, together with the honorable lords councilors, have summoned hereto the sergeant Jacob vander Veer, greetings.

Whereas Cornelis van Gezel has remonstrated to us how he, as plaintiff, requested in a suit on the 26th of October before the court in N. Amstel a sum of f143:8 stemming from excessive disbursements paid, loaned, and other monies due him, as per an account submitted to the defendant by law and also for this session; and also requested an account of some pieces of land paid for by Mr. d'Hinojossa for the late Mr. Alrichs (so he says), moreover, a conveyance on behalf of the estate on account of the pieces of land; and notwithstanding the mentioned payment was requested repeatedly outside the court, and accounts delivered and offered, nevertheless a copy was agreed to within 14 days; and on the 9th of November (although two special court sessions were held since then; also, the petitioner not knowing why he was being summoned by d'Hinojossa, waited until after midday; and also, he had requested to stand proxy, yet had to withdraw because nothing was done) the defendant first responded in session, making in addition a counter claim for the sum of f293:8:8 stemming [   ] from matters which the petitioner is not indebted; after this counter suit he also requested a copy of it in order to respond after due deliberation. Nevertheless the court pronounced in the same day a precipitous and mistaken judgment unjustly condemning the petitioner to a sum of ƒ134:11:8, where the matter was to have been closed for both suit and counter suit, without the petitioner having been able to receive from the secretary his own original papers in suit or the special marginal response of the defendant in counter suit or copies of the writs such as accounts, manuscripts and letters upon which the counter suit was based, but the same were improperly withheld by d'Hinojossa [   ] parties, so that the petitioner has not been able to proceed further as required; moreover, because he was ready to come here with the bark concerning the estate of the late Mr. Alrichs; above all this, d'Hinojossa has demanded the payment of the aforesaid sum of ƒ134:11:8 by a summons from the court messenger (so he says). For which reason he requests our assistance.

Therefore, we hereby order and commission you, Jacob vander Veer, upon the request of the aforesaid Cornelis van Gezel, to summon the aforementioned Alexander d'Hinojossa to come and to appear, or to send a deputy, before us here in Fort Amsterdam within the period of three weeks after announcement of this in order to sustain and vindicate the judgment and the contents thereof or to annul it; and, if it is so deemed, to respond to such demands and rejoinders as the aforesaid Van Gezel shall make and effect against him, inviting those of the aforesaid court (if it pleases them) to appear or to send deputies on the appointed day in order to see us annul or confirm the aforesaid judgment. Making copies for the parties and relating to us what you encounter.

Thus done and issued in Fort Amsterdam in N. Netherland, the 23rd of December 1660.

[16⁴:19]

[TEUNIS JANSZ APPEALS A JUDGMENT IN FAVOR OF MICHAEL TADENS]

Writ of Reduction*

Petrus Stuyvesandt, on behalf of their honorable High Mightinesses the lords States General of the United Netherlands and the lords directors of the Chartered West India Company, chamber of Amsterdam, director general of N. Netherland, Curaçao, Bonaire, Aruba and the dependencies thereof, together with the honorable lords councilors, have summoned hereto the court messenger, Claes van Elslant, greetings.

---

* Appeal of a judgment of arbitration.

Whereas Teunis Jansz, residing in the village of Breuckelen on Long Island, has shown us how he, petitioner, was accused of bad faith by Michiel Tadens, in that he, petitioner, cut a piece from the ear of each of two boar hogs belonging to him, Tadens, (so he said) and held them one and a half years; also, that the petitioner, contrary to the truth, sold one of them to Evert Duyckingh *Glaesemaker* during the last slaughtering season,* which according to Michiel Tadens would have been a white hog with black spots and an ear half cut off which was decorated. Whereupon Michiel Tadens threatened to summon the petitioner before the honorable court at Breuckelen; and he [   ] the petitioner through the strong advice of Albert Albertsz residing at Breuckel† and Salomon LaChair,‡ themselves offering to be arbitrators for the matter of the two boars in dispute, in order to settle by arbitration; and after they had made the petitioner afraid with threats that if the case came before the judge, it would not go well with him, together with other persuasive reasons, he, petitioner, let the aforesaid Albert Albertsz and Salomon LaChair persuade him because of his simple and shy nature (which could be presumed as a result of Michiel Tadens' request) to refer the dispute of the two boars to them. Their mistaken judgment was made on the 25th of July 1661, by which the petitioner finds himself greatly injured and harm done to his honor (so he says). For this reason he requests our assistance.§

Therefore, we hereby commission and order you to summon the aforesaid Michiel Tadens to appear, or to send deputies, before us here in Fort Amsterdam on the 25th of this month in order to see us annul and invalidate the aforesaid judgment, at least correcting and amending it, sustaining or repudiating it, as shall be deemed fit, inviting the aforesaid arbitrators to come on the appointed day, or to send deputies, if this matter concerns them in any way. Providing copies for the parties and relating to us what you encounter.

Thus done in Fort Amsterdam in New Netherland the 22nd of August 1661.**

---

* November
† village of Breuckelen on Long Island
‡ notary public in New Amsterdam
§ This judgment is no longer among the records.
** See NYCM, 9:731 and 740 for related proceedings of this appeal, dated 18 August 1661.

[16⁴:20]

[ADRIAEN BLOMMERT APPEALS A JUDGMENT
IN FAVOR OF MICHAEL JANSZ]

Petrus Stuyvesandt, on behalf of their honorable High Mightinesses the lords States General of the United Netherlands and the lords directors of the Chartered West India Company, chamber of Amsterdam, director general of N. Netherland, Curaçao, Bonaire, Aruba and the dependencies thereof, together with the honorable lords councilors, have summoned hereto the court messenger Claes van Elslant, greetings.

Whereas, Walewijn vander Veen,* in his capacity as deputy of Adriaen Blommert, has remonstrated to us by petition that he, in the aforesaid capacity, finds himself greatly injured and aggrieved by the judgment handed down by the magistrates of this city dated the first of October, last past, between him and Michiel Jansz for reasons detailed in the attached copy of the petition. For which reason he requests our assistance.†

Therefore, we order you to summon the aforesaid Michiel Jansz to appear, or to send a deputy, before us here in Fort Amsterdam in order to respond to such demands and rejoinders in addition to the appellant's petition to be exempt from the *indebite interjectie*‡ of his appeal which the aforesaid Walewijn vander Veen shall make and effect on the appointed day, inviting the aforesaid magistrates to appear or to send deputies at that time (if it pleases them) in order to see the judgment annulled or confirmed by us. Providing copies for the parties and relating to us what you encounter.§

Issued in Fort Amsterdam in New Netherland the 22d of December 1661.

---

* Vander Veen was a notary in New Amsterdam.

† Vander Veen had been awarded less money than he claimed in a debt suit against Michiel Jansz; see *RNA*, 3:368–69.

‡ intervening cost

§ The council upheld the judgment of the court of New Amsterdam; see NYCM, 10, part 1:11.

[16⁴:21]

[CORNELIS VAN LANGEVELDE APPEALS A JUDGMENT
IN FAVOR OF JANNEKE HEERMANS]

Petrus Stuyvesandt, on behalf of their honorable High Mightinesses the lords States General of the United Netherlands and the lords directors of the Chartered West India Company, chamber of Amsterdam, director general of N. Netherland, Curaçao, Bonaire, Aruba and the dependencies thereof, together with the honorable lords councilors, have summoned hereto the court messenger Claes van Elslant, greetings.

Whereas Cornelis van Langevelde has remonstrated to us by petition that he finds himself aggrieved and injured by the judgment handed down by the honorable court of this city, dated the first of October, last past, between him and Janneke Heermans for reasons stated in the attached copy of the petition. For which reason he requests our assistance.*

Therefore, we order you to summon the aforesaid Janneke Heermans to appear, or to send deputies, before us here in Fort Amsterdam in order to respond to such demands and rejoinders, in addition to the request of the appellant to be exempt from the intervening cost of his appeal, which the aforesaid Cornelis van Langevelde shall make and effect at that time, inviting those of the aforesaid court to appear (if it pleases them) on the aforementioned day, or to send deputies to see us annul or confirm the aforesaid judgment; providing copies for use of the parties, and relating to us what you encounter.†

Thus done and issued in Fort Amsterdam in New Netherland the 22d of December 1661.

[16⁴:22]

[JACOBUS VIS APPEALS A JUDGMENT IN FAVOR OF
ISAAC VERMEULEN]

Petrus Stuyvesandt, on behalf of their honorable High Mightinesses the lords States General of the United Netherlands and the lords directors of the Chartered West India Company, chamber of Amsterdam, director

---

* Van Langevelde had been ordered to return the pearl earrings which Janneke Heermans claimed she had given to Balthus Loockermans to sell at Fort Orange. See *RNA*, 3:369.
† The council ordered Van Langevelde either to return the pearls or money equal to the value of the pawn; see NYCM, 10¹:20.

general of N. Netherland, Curaçao, Bonaire, Aruba and the dependencies thereof, together with the honorable lords councilors, have summoned hereto the court messenger, Claes van Elslant, greetings.

Whereas Jacobus Vis has remonstrated to us by petition that he finds himself greatly injured and aggrieved by the judgment handed down by the honorable court of this city dated 14 September, last past, between him and Isaacq Vermeulen for reasons detailed in the attached copy of the petition. For which reason he requests our assistance.*

Therefore, we order you to summon the aforesaid Isaacq Vermeulen, or his deputy, to appear, or to send a deputy, before us here in Fort Amsterdam on Thursday being the 26th of this month to respond to such demands and rejoinders, in addition to the appellant's request to be exempt from the intervening costs of his appeal, which the aforesaid Jacobus Vis shall make and effect at that time, inviting those of the aforesaid court to appear (if it pleases them) on the aforementioned day, or to send deputies to see us annul or confirm the aforesaid judgment; providing copies for use of the parties, and relating to us what you encounter.†

Issued in Fort Amsterdam in New Netherland,
the 12th of January 1662.

[16⁴:23]

[JACOBUS VIS APPEALS A JUDGMENT IN FAVOR OF HANS STEYN]

Petrus Stuyvesandt, on behalf of their honorable High Mightinesses the lords States General of the United Netherlands and the lords directors of the Chartered West India Company, chamber of Amsterdam, director general of N. Netherland, Curacao, Bonaire, Aruba and the dependencies thereof, together with the honorable lords councilors, have summoned hereto the court messenger, Claes van Elslant, greetings.

Whereas Jacobus Vis has remonstrated to us by petition that he finds himself greatly injured and aggrieved by the judgment handed down by

---

* Vermeulen had sued Vis for back payment for his services, which Vis claimed was not owed. The court ordered Vis to reimburse Vermeulen; see *RNA*, 3:356–57 for this order.

† The council upheld the judgment of the court of New Amsterdam; see NYCM, 10¹:24.

the honorable court of this city dated 13 December, last past, between him and Hans Steyn for reasons detailed in the attached copy of the petition. For which he requests our assistance.*

Therefore, we order you to summon the aforesaid Hans Steyn to appear, or to send a deputy, before us here in Fort Amsterdam on Thursday being the 26th of this month in order to respond to such demands and rejoinders which the aforesaid Jacobus Vis shall make and effect at that time, inviting those of the aforesaid court to appear (if it pleases them) on the aforementioned day, or to send deputies to see us annul or confirm the aforesaid judgment; providing copies for use of the parties, and relating to us what you encounter.†

Issued in Fort Amsterdam in New Netherland, the 12th of January 1662.

[16⁴:24]

[WESSEL EVERTSEN APPEALS A JUDGMENT IN FAVOR OF FRANS JANSEN VAN HOCHTEN]

Petrus Stuyvesandt, on behalf of their honorable High Mightinesses the lords States General of the United Netherlands and the lords directors of the Chartered West India Company, chamber of Amsterdam, director general of N. Netherland, Curaçao, Bonaire, Aruba and the dependencies thereof, together with the honorable lords councilors, have summoned hereto the court messenger, Claes van Elslant, greetings.

Whereas Wessel Evertsz has remonstrated to us that he finds himself greatly aggrieved by the judgment of the arbitrators concerning the matter in dispute between the aforesaid Wessel Evertsz and Frans Jansen van Hochten, carpenter, appended to the judgment of the honorable burgomasters and *schepenen* of this city, dated 31 January, last past, as appears in more detail by his petition attached hereto.‡ For which he requests our assistance.

---

* The court upheld the judgment of arbitrators Tymotheus Gabry and Joannes van Brugh who had decided that Vis was to pay Steyn a certain balance in their account, plus court costs. See *RNA*, 3:426.

† Though the council minutes for this case are damaged, it would appear that the council upheld the court's decision; see NYCM, 10¹:24.

‡ Wessel Evertsz had been ordered to pay Frans Jansen for work done on Evertsz' house. Evertsz maintained it was not completed; Jansen maintained he had done all that was ordered. Arbitrators Nicolas de Meyer and Robert Rolans decided in favor of Jansen, the defendant; see *RNA*, 4:24–25. The council's decision is not known.

Therefore, we order you to summon the aforesaid Frans Jansen van Hochten to appear, or to send a deputy, before us here in Fort Amsterdam, on Thursday being the 23rd of this month, in order to see us annul and vacate the aforesaid judgment, at least correcting and emending it, sustaining or repudiating it, as shall be deemed fit; in addition, responding to such demands which the petitioner shall make at that time to be exempt from the intervening costs of his arbitration and appeal, inviting the aforesaid magistrates, together with the arbitrators stated in the attached petition, to appear or to send deputies, on the appointed day (if it pleases them), ordering, on behalf of the high authorities of this province, the aforesaid defendant and concerned parties to do or effect nothing in prejudice of the aforesaid arbitration and appeal, rather, on the contrary, if anything were done or effected to reinstate it at once without delay, and to return it to its original and proper state. Providing copies on behalf of the parties and relating to us what you encounter.

Thus done and issued in Fort Amsterdam in N. Netherland, the 14th of March 1662.

[16^4:25]*

[JERONIMUS EBBINGE APPEALS A JUDGMENT IN FAVOR OF CORNELIS BARENTS SLECHT]

Petrus Stuyvesandt, on behalf of their honorable High Mightinesses the lords States General of the United Netherlands and the lords directors of the Chartered West India Company, chamber of Amsterdam, director general of N. Netherland, Curaçao, Bonaire, Aruba and the dependencies thereof, together with the honorable lords councilors, have summoned hereto the court messenger of the inferior court of justice in the village of Wiltwijck, greetings.†

Whereas Jeronimus Ebbinge has remonstrated to us by petition that he finds himself greatly injured and aggrieved by the judgment handed down by the honorable court of the village of Wiltwijck in the Esopus, dated 28 March, last past, between him and Cornelis Baerents Slecht for

---

* Although this document is listed as number 26 in O'Callaghan's calendar, it is actually marked 16^4:25. There is no 16^4:26.

† The court of Wiltwijck was established in 1661. Under the English this community in the mid Hudson Valley was renamed Kingston. Previously the entire region was under the jurisdiction of the court of Fort Orange. At this time and long after the establishment of Wiltwijck the region was known as the Esopus.

reasons detailed in the attached copy of the petition. For which he requests our assistance.*

Therefore, we order and command you to summon the aforesaid Cornelis Baerents Slecht to appear before us here in Fort Amsterdam on Thursday, being the 27th of this month, in order to respond to such demands and rejoinders which the aforesaid Jeronimus Ebbinge shall make and effect at that time, inviting also those of the aforesaid court to appear or send deputies on the appointed day, if it pleases them, in order to see the aforesaid judgment annulled or confirmed by us. Providing copies on behalf of the parties and relating to us what you encounter.

Issued in Fort Amsterdam in New Netherland the 16th of April 1662.

[16^4:27]

[TOBIAS FEAKE APPEALS A JUDGMENT IN FAVOR OF WILLIAM HALLET]

Petrus Stuyvesant director general of New Netherland, together with the honorable councilors, has summoned hereto the court messenger, Claes van Elslant, greetings.

Whereas Tobias Feake, resident of *Vlissingen* on Long Island, has remonstrated to us by petition that he finds himself greatly injured and aggrieved by the judgment handed down by the honorable court of the village of Vlissingen, dated 5 April, last past,† between him and William Hallet for reasons detailed in the attached copy of the petition. For which he requests our assistance.

Therefore, we order and command you to summon the aforesaid William Hallet to appear or to send a deputy before us here in Fort Amsterdam on Thursday, being the 18th of this month in order to respond to such demands and rejoinders which the aforesaid Tobias Feake shall make and effect against him at that time, inviting also those of the aforesaid court to appear or to send deputies on the appointed day (if it pleases them) in order to see us annul or confirm the aforesaid judgment. Proving copies on behalf of the parties and relating what you encounter.‡

---

*   Ebbing was requesting the return of his farm which was leased to Slecht, and the lease, which the Wiltwijck court refused. The council, however, granted Ebbing's appeal. See *NYHM, Kingston Papers*, 1:26 and NYCM, 10^1: 121.

†   These records no longer exist.

‡   There is no record of the council's decision.

Issued in Fort Amsterdam in New Netherland the 4th of May 1662.

[16⁴:28]

[JERONIMUS EBBINGE APPEALS A JUDGMENT IN FAVOR OF PHILIP PIETERSEN SCHUYLER AND PIETER HARTGERS]

Petrus Stuyvesandt, on behalf of their honorable High Mightinesses the lords States General of the United Netherlands and the lords directors of the Chartered West India Company, chamber of Amsterdam, director general of N. Netherland, Curaçao, Bonaire, Aruba and the dependencies thereof, together with the honorable lords councilors, has summoned hereto the court messenger, Lodovicus Cobes, greetings.

Whereas Jeronimus Ebbinge has remonstrated to us by petition that he finds himself greatly aggrieved by the judgment handed down by the honorable court of Fort Orange and the village of Beverwijck, dated 14 March, last past, between Philip Pietersen Schuyler's deputy Gerrit Swart and Abraham Staats, the deputy of Pieter Hartgers, for reasons detailed in the attached copy of the petition. For which our assistance is requested.*

Therefore, we order you to summon the aforesaid Gerrit Swart and Abraham Staats to appear, or to send deputies, before us here at Fort Amsterdam on a designated, suitable day in order to respond to such demands and rejoinders which the petitioner shall make at that time, in addition to his request to be exempt from the intervening costs of his appeal, inviting also those of the aforesaid court to appear, or to send deputies, on the appointed day (if it pleases them) in order to see us annul, correct or confirm the aforesaid judgment. Providing copies on behalf of the parties and relating to us what you encounter.†

Issued in Fort Amsterdam in New Netherland the 5th of June 1662.

---

* The Fort Orange court records for this period are missing.
† There is no record of the council's decision.

[16⁴:29]

[WRIT EMPOWERING MARRITGEN ABRAHAMS TO ADMINISTER
THE ESTATE OF HER LATE HUSBAND TOMAS JANSZ MINGAEL
UNDER BENEFIT OF INVENTORY]

The director general and council of New Netherland, to all who shall see
this or hear it read, greetings.

Let it be known that we have received the humble petition of Marritgen
Abrahams, widow, and Abraham Pietersz *Moolenaer* father-in-law of
Tomas Jansz Mingael, deceased now about three weeks, and that the
possessions he left behind from an intestate have devolved upon his three
minority children, and because the petitioners, mother and grandfather,
hence guardians of the aforesaid three children, are concerned that the
estate of her deceased husband and his son-in-law might be burdened
with many debts, so that the simple acceptance of it might be detrimental
to the petitioners, they find it not advisable to accept the same estate
except under benefit of inventory (so they the petitioners say). For which
reason they request with all due humility that their case be favored and
expedited by our open letter to such effect.

Therefore, we have deliberated the aforesaid matter and being in favor
of the petitioners' request, we have allowed and permitted the petitioners,
as we hereby allow and permit, our letter, which they, the petitioners,
may carry under benefit of inventory and place heirs in the aforesaid
house of the deceased Tomas Jansz Mingal, and in this capacity take
possession and enter upon the same house of the deceased, and the
possessions, chattels, securities, debits and credits left behind by the
aforesaid Tomas Jansz Mingael, on the condition that a good and honest
inventory be made by one of the officers of the district where most of
the possessions of the deceased are located, selecting the one who is most
appropriate in such matters; and provided that the petitioners be
obligated to post good and sufficient bond and security to pay for all the
debts, bequests and legacies of the aforesaid deceased as far as the
possessions may cover, without the petitioners being obligated in any
way to pay anything above the value thereof; unless there still be a
relative of the deceased who has simply installed himself or intends to
install himself as heir, then summon and order the officer of the city of
Amsterdam in New Netherland and also all other magistrates and officers, or their deputies, each one as far as it may concern him, that the
aforesaid inventory be honestly completed and the security posted by the
petitioners, and received and registered by the secretary of the aforesaid
city; making sure that the petitioners are delivered of all assignable and

inheritable possessions left behind by the aforesaid Tomas Jansz Mingael, and allowing them to enjoy and use in peace and freedom the contents of this our present benefit of inventory in the aforesaid manner and under the aforesaid limitations and modifications, without causing them any impediments or trouble; on the contrary, we hereby summon, command and commission our court messenger (hereto requested by the aforesaid petitioners) to go to the persons or residences of all creditors of the aforesaid house of the deceased, who are certain and known, in addition to the beneficiaries, as far as there are any, and to summon them on behalf of the high authorities of this province to appear, or to send deputies, before the court of the aforementioned city, where the house of the deceased is located, on a certain suitable day, which he shall indicate to them, in order to see, there or wherever necessary, all the possessions (left behind by the aforesaid Tomas Jansz Mingal) properly inventoried and to see them appraised according to the ordinance and the contents of this, and to post security by the aforesaid petitioners as is appropriate. At the same time we hereby commission the aforesaid court messenger, at the request of the aforesaid petitioners, to summon and invite by public edict or proclamation, at the place where notices are usually posted, the other equivocal and unknown creditors, if there be any, and all others who shall in any way impugn this letter of benefit of inventory and oppose it and those who were to install themselves as creditors and beneficiaries of the aforesaid Tomas Jansz Mingal, authorizing and commissioning him hereby to summon and cite all the same creditors and beneficiaries, and all others who are in opposition, either by edict or summoned and invited by other means, to appear, or to send deputies, before the court of the aforesaid city of Amsterdam in N. Netherland in order to see the aforesaid writ of benefit of inventory approved by them or to speak against the same, with notification if they appear or send deputies; if not, then proceedings shall still be instituted by the aforesaid court for confirmation of the aforesaid writ of benefit of inventory, as otherwise according to law. He is to relate his encounters with those of the aforesaid court whom we hereby expressly commission (having heard the parties) to execute justice in a swift and equitable manner.

Thus done and issued, and confirmed with our seal in red wax impressed thereon in Fort Amsterdam in New Netherland the [*left blank*].*

---

* While there is no date on this copy, the widow and her father appeared before the court of New Amsterdam on January 9, 1663, with letters of benefit of inventory from the council dated January 2, 1663. See *RNA*,4 :178–79.

[16⁴:30]

[JAN CULPEPER APPEALS A JUDGMENT
IN FAVOR OF HATTON ATKINS]

The honorable director general and council of New Netherland have summoned hereto the court messenger Claes van Elslant, greetings.

Whereas Jan Culpeper has remonstrated to us by petition that he finds himself greatly aggrieved by a certain decision of the honorable court of this city dated the 22d of this month, granted at his request on the matter in contention between him, petitioner, and one Hatton Atkins for reasons detailed in the attached copy of the petition. For which our assistance is requested.*

Therefore, we order [you] to summon the aforesaid Hatton Atkins to appear or to send a deputy, before us here in Fort Amsterdam, on Monday, being the 28th of this month, in order to respond to such demands and rejoinders which the aforesaid Jan Culpeper shall make and effect against him at that time, inviting also those of the aforesaid court to appear, or tosend deputies, on the appointed day (if it pleases them) in order to see us confirm or alter the aforesaid decision. Providing copies on behalf of the parties and relating to us what you encounter.

Done in Fort Amsterdam in New Netherland,
the 29th of May 1663.

[16⁴:31]

[PIETER TONNEMAN APPEALS A JUDGMENT IN FAVOR OF
ANDRIES REES AND ANDRIES JOCHEMSZ]

The honorable director general and council of New Netherland have summoned hereto the court messenger, Claes van Elslant, greetings.

Whereas the honorable Pieter Tonneman, *schout* of this city, has remonstrated to us by petition that he found himself greatly aggrieved by the judgment handed down by the honorable court of this city dated 26 June, last past, between him and Andries Rees and Andries Jochemsz for

---

* This was Culpeper's second appeal from the judgment of the New Amsterdam court's decision regarding his account with Atkins. The council, having rejected Culpeper's first appeal, ruled in favor of Atkins. See NYCM, 10²:81, 111– 12, 116, 119 for the rulings of the council; and *RNA*, 4:226, 228, 230–31, 241, 245 for the progress of the case in the court of New Amsterdam.

reasons detailed in the attached copy of the petition. For this our assistance is requested.*

Therefore, we order you to summon the aforesaid Andries Rees and Andries Jochemsz to appear, or to send a deputy, before us here in Fort Amsterdam on Thursday being the 12th of this month in order to respond to such demands and rejoinders which the aforesaid *schout*, Pieter Tonneman, shall make or effect on that day, inviting also those of the aforesaid court (if it pleases them) to appear, or to send deputies on the appointed day in order to see us annul or confirm the aforesaid judgment. Providing copies on behalf of the parties and relating to us what you encounter.

Issued in Fort Amsterdam in New Netherland the 9th of July 1663.

[16⁴:32]

[RELEASE OF CHRISTINA STEENGENS FROM ALL DEBTS INCURRED BY HER LATE HUSBAND]

Petrus Stuyvesant, on behalf of their honorable High Mightinesses the lords states general of the United Netherlands and the honorable lords directors of the Chartered West India Company, chamber at Amsterdam, director general of N. Netherland, Curaçao etc., together with the honorable lords councilors, our dear and faithful magistrates of the city of Amsterdam in N. Netherland, greetings.

If (summoned those who warrant being summoned hereto) it would appear to you that Cristina Steentgens, widow of Gabriel de Haes, residing in aforesaid Amsterdam, intends to cede and resign from all her possessions for the profit of her creditors, therefore, in such event, we hereby summon and order you [   ] to receive [   ] Christina Steentgen's (debts [   ]honestly known) without deceit; to do the aforesaid cession in the customary manner and having done the said cession [   ] her peacefully and tranquilly enjoy and use without troubling or bothering her about the cause of the aforesaid debts or letting her be troubled or bothered in any way; but if she were imprisoned, it would represent or be represented as a complete exoneration, notwithstanding some promis-

---

* Tonneman cited Rees for allowing people to game and drink on Sunday at his house, contrary to the ordinance. Rees's defense, that he tapped two hours after the afternoon sermon, was allowed and he was not fined. The council's decision regarding the judgment is not known. See *RNA*, 4:264 for this case.

sory notes or bonds and surreptitious papers to the contrary, disregarding the debts still due the high authorities;and besides, if she afterwards were to come into a fortune of goods, she would be obligated to satisfy her aforesaid creditors, and because the aforesaid Christina Steentgens's creditors reside at Amsterdam in Holland, beyond our jurisdiction, it is requested by petition of the aforesaid Cristina Steentgens, for the sake of justice, that a sworn court messenger at Amsterdam summon all the [   ] ceded creditors and creditors to come and appear or to send representatives for your honor on the 2nd Thursday in the month of July 1664, being the 10th day of the same month, in order to see the papers of cession presented by the ceded creditors, and to request confirmation of them, requesting on the contrary, if they see fit to continue, then arrange matters accordingly; and he, court messenger, shall have done herein [   ] on the aforesaid day in order that [   ] (parties having been heard) right and justice may be done accordingly with the aforesaid cession. Done at Fort Amsterdam in N. Netherland the 1st of October 1663.*

Unpaid.

---

* On September 10, 1663, Christiana Steentgens had petitioned for a writ to allow her to surrender her husband's estate for the benefit of his creditors. See NYCM, 10^2:295.

Appendix

Copy from
the minutes

> Inventory made by Thomas Robijn Duerwaer-
> der of the High Council in Holland, done by
> virtue of certain open letters of benefit of
> inventory, dated the eleventh of March 1664,
> of the aforesaid high council obtained by Cor-
> nelis van Gaezel, executor, together with Ca-
> tharina Ram and Pieter Alrix, the heirs of
> Jacob Alrix, in his lifetime director general of
> the colony New Amstel in New Netherland,
> procurers of the aforesaid benefit of inventory,
> and that in the presence of Cornelis De Grijp,
> notary public here, as especially commis-
> sioned hereto by the court of Amsterdam, the
> aforesaid procurers declare such goods, move-
> able and immoveable, securities and credits
> left behind and bequeathed by the deceased at
> his death.

On the 12th of May 1664, the clock having struck 12 o'clock, being the
prearranged day and hour to proceed with the inventory and estimate of
the aforesaid goods, I, the aforementioned Duerwaarde, with the aforementioned commissioner of the aforesaid court and the aforesaid pro-
curers, except for the aforesaid Pieter Alrix, because of his absence from
the country, appeared at the house of Cornelis van Gaesel, located and
situated on the Haarlemmerdijck, on the corner of the Eenhoorens Sluys,
in the city of Amsteldam, which served as the death house.

Having arrived there, and having heard from none of the creditors, I
began to inventory and appraise the aforesaid goods as follows:

A certain folio writing book bound in a calf's leather binding, entitled Memorandum of receipts and disbursements of the year 1654 for the chartered West India Company, marked No. 1.

A bundle of papers concerning claims on behalf of the West India Company, marked No. 2.

Memorandum of goods left by the deceased *Heer* with Gasper van Huesen, and because the same has deceased, now reposing with Coenraaten Hendrik van Huesen, with all the papers pertaining thereto, marked No. 3.

Four bonds on behalf of Willem Bex concerning some animal, with the conveyance and letter accompanying it, marked No. 4.

A bond, judgment and other accounts relating to Do. Johannes Theodorus Polhemius, marked No. 5.

A reckoning of monthly salaries, with accompanying accounts, concerning Hans Croeger, on behalf of the aforementioned Company, marked No. 6.

Some papers regarding claims on behalf of Huibert Brest, marked No. 8

A bundle of papers coming from the estate of the deceased Dortmondt, marked No. 9

An inventory of papers sorted into thirty-seven bundles, identified with the letters ABC etc. concerning the administration of the deceased relating to the South River, marked No. 10.

Inventory of furniture and household furnishings seized in New Netherland, marked No. 11.

Inventory of real estate, together with interests and claims in Brazil, marked No. 12.

Some papers relating to interests in Embderlandt, marked No. 13.

Some papers of real estate in New Netherland, marked No.14.

Some papers concerning private people, marked No. 15.

Some other papers of little value, marked No. 16.

Five plates decorated with pen and with teakwood.

Forty-five carved [engraved] coconuts, whole and broken.

Two cotton hammocks.

Some old books, maps and prints of little value.

A gold weight of teakwood.

A standing table clock, being the same one valued by a clock maker at sixty guilders; still to be found at the house of *Sr*. Willem van Ghezel, as follows:

Eight bound books in folio.

Ten ditto books in quarto.

And another parcel of small books valued and appraised in proportion with the aforesaid eighteen, and previously stated old books, maps and prints of little value, after an examination by the underwritten Jan van Doesburgh, book seller here, for the sum of seventy guilders; was signed Jan van Duisberg.

Also to be found at the aforesaid house: a large quantity of papers, lying in a trunk next to the aforementioned books, which was declared to be of little value.

A large, old world map.

A large Brazil chest with some boxes.

And the aforesaid Cornelis van Ghaezel, procurer hereof, declares that the aforementioned goods have been inventoried to the best of his knowledge and in good conscience [   ]. In testimony hereof the aforesaid procurer and security has signed this on the 12th of May 1664; was signed Cornelis van Gezel.

[DEPOSITION OF HENDRIK GERRITSZ VAN GHEESEL CONCERNING
THE DEATH OF JACOB ALRICHS]

Appeared before me, Cornelis de Grijp etc., the honorable Hendrik Gerritsz van Gheesel, about 48 years old, former court messenger of the colony of New Amstel in New Netherland, as indicated to me, notary, by his passport, while present here and at the request of *Sr*. Cornelis van Ghaezel, former secretary there, witnessed, declared and testified with true words, in place of a solemn oath, offered upon request, to be true, truthful and to him, attester, to be certain and well known that which follows:

1. First, that the *Heer* Jacob Alrichs, director of the aforesaid colony while alive, departed this world on the 30th day of December 1659 in the morning hours.

2. That he, attester, received an order the same morning from Allexander de Hinoyossa, then lieutenant there, to call a meeting for the same morning, which he, attester, did. At which time he, Allexander de Hinoyossa, assisted or accompanied by Gerrit van Sweeringhe, *schout* there, took possession of and seized the room where the aforesaid *Heer* Alrichs, deceased, had passed away, together with everything that was in it; likewise, they had their bedclothes also brought to them, and spent the night there.

3. Likewise, he, attester, was ordered by Hinoyossa to call a meeting the following day, and one day after the other for several days in a row.

4. That also one or two days after the burial of the departed *Heer* Alrichs, he, the petitioner, was locked out of the fort by the aforesaid Hinoyossa who ordered the gates closed between 5 and 6 o'clock in the evening; ordinarily they closed at 9 o'clock, and the following day they were not opened again until eight thirty, without being willing to let him, attester, in that evening, notwithstanding that he was informed that the petitioner was standing before the gate and requested permission to enter. Thus he, the petitioner, had to stay outside that night.

5. That also the aforesaid All. de Hinoyossa took possession of the animals and farms belonging to the aforesaid deceased *Heer* Alrichs, and leased the bare land to a certain Heye Ykes; and he used the servants in his service. Some of the animals, he, All. de Hinoyossa, turned over to Swedes or Finns on certain conditions.

6. That also he, attester, heard and understood from the mouth of Abraham van Nas that All. de Hinoyossa, shortly after the death of the aforesaid *Heer* Alrichs, when a dispute had arisen between him, the petitioner, and Hinoyossa, had offered him, Van Nas, the petitioner's office of secretary, adding that we shall not be able to expect any more service from Van Ghaezel.

7. That also he, attester, shortly thereafter was ordered by the aforesaid Alexander de Hinoyossa to go to the petitioner and inform him that he is not to leave the fort until further orders.

8. That also he, attester, was ordered by the aforesaid Alexander de Hinoyossa, [to inform] him, the petitioner, that the council requested his appearance there, which he, the petitioner refused, saying that he did not

know what he would do there since one let other people take care of his positions and offices, namely, Johannes Crato as councillor and Gerrit van Sweeringhe as secretary, about which he, attester, informed Alexander de Hinoyossa. He was again sent with instructions to notify him, the petitioner, that the same had indeed happened in matters concerning the Colony, but not in matters of justice or civil suits, and therefore, he would have to appear in the council. For this he, the petitioner, excused himself, saying that there were some pressing matters to take care of and being unable to come.

9. That also he, attester, shortly thereafter was ordered by the aforesaid Alexander de Hinoyossa to go to the petitioner's house with the *schout's* servant (the petitioner being at Fort Altena) in order to execute attachment concerning a certain *f*25 fine, for refusing orders to take an oath, for which they took a mirror and a small painting against the will of the petitioner's wife, leaving there at his house another order to appear at the council meeting the following morning in order to take the oath upon a fine of *f*50; and they brought the aforesaid mirror and small painting to the *schout's* house, which shortly thereafter (the petitioner having come home) were placed back in his hands.

10. That he, attester, also heard and learned several times that the aforesaid Alexander de Hinoyossa had threatened to send him, the petitioner, back to the fatherland.

11. That it was also well known to him, the attester, that on several occasions a council meeting was held concerning some murdered Indians, without the petitioner being summoned, but that he, attester, was sent to the petitioner's house for the protocol, which he, the petitioner, himself brought, and then left again, hearing that he, the petitioner, was not at all happy about it, and, among other things, said to the aforesaid Alexander de Hinoyossa, "I think that you should just stay home and call council meetings there as you find convenient."

12. That he, attester, was ordered into the petitioner's house by the aforesaid Alexander de Hinoyossa in order to guard the goods in the house and to take care that none of the same would be taken out of there, where he, attester, also was to stay and sleep.

13. That he, attester, heard and understood from the aforesaid Abraham van Nas that the aforementioned Alexander de Hinoyossa urged Van Nas to see to it that he be paid the nine hundred guilders that he was to have from the estate of the deceased *Heer* Alrix through Cornelis van Ghaesel, the petitioner, as executor and heir in this under benefit of inventory; that

everything would then be fine, and they would be friends; and that he, Van Nas, would receive from him, Alexander de Hinoyossa, one hundred guilders for it, which payment of ƒ900 he, attester, also understood did take place; and that he also knew for a fact that some barrels of wheat flour had been involved, however, he, Alexander de Hinoyossa, later refused to make good on the aforesaid ƒ100 for the abovementioned Van Nas, which is still a matter of dispute.

14. That it is also true that he, attester, at the request of Alexander de Hinoyossa received and enjoyed from the deceased *Heer* Alrichs's estate some musk-colored cloth with appertenances for a dress as compensation for services rendered with the Swedes and elsewhere in the service of the colony performed at the time of *Heer* Alrichs, deceased.

15. That it is well known to him, attester, that Alexander de Hinoyossa, in spite of the fact that he had confiscated almost all the effects of the deceased *Heer* Alrichs for himself, nevertheless would tell all the creditors and claimants on the aforesaid estate that they had to go to the petitioner, Cornelis van Ghaesel, if they had any claims to make.

16. That he, attester, also heard, and it was common knowledge there, that Gerrit van Sweeringhen had taken all the books and papers of the deceased *Heer* Alrichs with him to the fatherland (while the petitioner was at the Manatans).

17. That he, attester, had also heard at various times from Matthijs Capito, who had come there from Manatans to draw up the accounts, and the aforesaid Capito said to him, attester, in a complaining manner that he could not proceed with drawing up the accounts because one document or the other was lacking; and that the aforementioned Alexander de Hinoyossa sent him, attester, to the aforesaid Capito, requesting this and that paper (being one number or the other), which he, attester, then brought and handed over to the aforementioned Alexander de Hinoyossa, whereupon Matthijs Capito finally departed because, as he said, he was unable to obtain or gain access to those accounts and documents that were necessary for drawing up the accounts.

18. That he, attester, at various times and from various persons heard and learned that the petitioner had been among some Swedes or Finns, who had acquired from the aforementioned Alexander de Hinoyossa some cows belonging to the deceased *Heer* Alrichs's farm by a certain contract as stated above, and had spoken to them about the aforementioned livestock; when the same Swedes and Finns [informed] Alexander de

Hinoyossa about it, he supposedly told them "if he, Van Ghaezel, comes among you people again, you can just shoot him dead."

19. He, attester, further declares that on the 10th of June in 1661 (as the petitioner was intending to depart for Manatans with the galiot *Nieuwer Amstel*, skippered by Jacob Jansz Huys, and all his goods were on board) he arrested the petitioner by order of Alexander de Hinoyossa, and he, Alexander de Hinoyossa, made it necessary for him, the petitioner, to appear at the Manatans on penalty of ƒ600, and he had to travel to that place overland at great expense and danger.

20. That he, attester, also knows with certainty that on Pinxter day* in the year 1661, when the sermon and divine service had concluded, and he, the petitioner, had stood up, the aforementioned Alexander de Hinoyossa had the petitioner's chair, which stood in the church and in which the petitioner was accustomed to sit, removed from its place and taken out of the church by a servant of the *schout*, and sent the chair to the petitioner's house.

21. That he, attester, on the 23d of August 1661, in the name and by order of Alexander de Hinoyossa, was at the petitioner's house (the petitioner being at Fort Altena), and impounded all the petitoner's goods and effects, ordering the petitioner's wife to open the chests in order to see what goods were in there or that she could otherwise use to post the security of ƒ1,000; whereupon the petitioner's wife requested 24 hours' time to inform her husband of the matter, which was reported to Alexander de Hinoyossa and he refused. Whereupon the petitioner's wife left, saying she was going to inquire about security. In the meanwhile, he, attester, was ordered by Alexander de Hinoyossa, to take a hammer with a claw back there; and arriving at the petitioner's house with Pieter Pietersz Harder, councilor and Reynier Ravens, clerk, and finding no one home, broke out a window, opened the door, opened the chests, and inventoried the goods. In the meantime the petitioner's wife returned home and found the people there busy at work. When she wanted to take some children's things to use for her child, the aforesaid Pieter Pietersz Harder pushed her away very disrespectfully, saying she had no business there and to go away. He forced her, furthermore, to hand over the other keys, threatening to break more things to pieces. He, attester, and the aforementioned clerk (everything having been inventoried) remained there through the night by special order of Alexander de Hinoyossa, after

* Pentecost, or Whitsunday, the seventh Sunday after Easter commemorating the descent of the Holy Spirit on the apostles.

summoning the attester and ordering him to inform the petitioner's wife that she was to come to him at the fort; however, he, attester, did not find her at home and was unable to deliver the message.

22. Whereupon he, Alexander de Hinoyossa, ordered the attester and Reynier Ravens to proclaim by striking the cymbal that the petitioner was a bankrupt and fugitive, and that no one should undertake to lodge or quarter the petitioner's wife or any goods, and for all those who had quartered the aforesaid wife or goods, that they should at once step forward and make it known, upon arbitrary punishment, and by failure to do so, that their houses would be searched, which striking of cymbals and commotion was done by the attester, and the proclamation or written publication instituted by Alexander de Hinoyossa, was done by Reynier Ravens, aforesaid, by order of the aforementioned Alexander de Hinoyossa.

23. After all of which no information was forthcoming, the aforementioned Alexander de Hinoyossa went out in person with the aforesaid Pieter Pietersz den Harder, the attester with two soldiers, and conducted house searches, and posted soldiers in all the passageways and roads in order to catch the petitioner's wife. He, the attester, learned from the inhabitants there, that, on account of such close pursuit, it was necessary for the petitioner's wife to abandon her frail baby of four months, and, out of fear, to hide it in the woods. The child afterwards was revealed and brought before the public by a certain Mari Karmans who claimed to have found it by a fence, whereupon Alexander de Hinoyossa ordered the attester to place it in the custody of the aforesaid woman, and went there himself to the same Maria Karmans, ordering her to take good care of it and not to hand it over to anyone, or he would hold her responsible for it. To this Mari Karmans said that because she had to look after her own children and had her own things to do, she was unable to comply, but would rather hand the child over to him, Alexander de Hinoyossa. Whereupon the child was brought to him and given to the attester's wife, who lived in the fort, to take care of, provided that he would pay for it. However, if she did not take good care of it and let it be taken from her, then she would receive no payment for her troubles. But because the attester's wife was not nursing, the child was often brought outside the fort to be nursed by the aforesaid Mari Karmans. While bringing it to be nursed, the child was taken away by someone hired by the petitioner. During the confinement of the child, the petitioner, who was given shelter at Fort Altena, where the attester by order of Alexander de Hinoyossa also executed attachment proceedings on everything belong-

ing to his wife (who had fled there to him) by means of a letter to the *Heer* Willem Beekman, vice director of the West India Company there, having heard of this, sent Andries Hudde to the aforementioned Alexander de Hinoyossa, and requested the return of the child, which Alexander de Hinoyossa refused to do, the attester hearing among other words spoken to the aforesaid Hudde, "I really give a damn!" Whereupon the aforesaid child was taken away, as already stated.

24. Furthermore, Alexander de Hinoyossa, upon learning that the petitioner intended to depart for the fatherland, summoned him by ringing the bell, forbidding all bark skippers from transporting him with any vessel.

25. Finally, the attestant declares that it was well known to him that Gerrit van Sweeringhe at the end of the year 1659, without knowing the precise month or date, at the time that he left his position as commissary of the magazine, and was to hand over all the magazine's effects to the petitioner; however, removed three boxes of magazine's goods, and took them with his own [goods]. These three boxes of magazine's goods, which were later at the beginning of the year 1660 taken out of Van Sweringhe's house, contained the same goods: all sorts of clothing and accompanying items such as caps, stockings, shirts, buttons, and other things; also, a parcel of carpenter's tools and other things. In conclusion the attester declares all the substance of his testimony to be true and truthful. Thus done within Amsterdam in the presence of Lucas Brouwer and Abraham de Ghraaf as witnesses etc.,
this 2d of August 1662.

Hendrick Gerritsz van Geseel
Lucas Brouwer
A. d. Ghraaf

Quod attestor
C. de Ghrijp, n. pub.

[DEPOSITION OF HENDRIK VAN BIJLEVELT
CONCERNING THE DEATH OF J. ALRICHS]

Appeared before me Cornelis de Grijp etc. the honorable Hendrik van Bijlevelt, 40 years' old, having served as corporal of soldiers in the colony New Amstel in New Netherland in the service of the honorable lords burgomasters of this city, presently residing here, and has deposed, declared and testified at the request of *Sr*. Cornelis van Ghaezel, former secretary in New Netherland, how true and truthful it is that he, attester, after the death of the deceased *Heer* Jacob Alricx, heard Allexander de Hinoyossa greatly slander the deceased *Heer*, and accuse him in front of the attester and other soldiers of bad administration of the colony. He declared further that he was well aware that the petitioner, shortly after the death of the aforementioned *Heer* Alricx, deceased, on a certain day (without knowing the precise time or day, or wanting to be obligated to it) went outside the gate of the fort New Amstel, Allexander de Hinoyossa had the gate of the fort closed at about five o'clock in the evening, which otherwise was closed at nine o'clock, and that he, the petitioner, came before the same gate about half past five, requesting permission to be let inside, about which the sentry was informed by the sergeant and together with the petitioner's wife [   ] requested of the aforementioned Hinoyossa, who refused to do so, but kept the aforesaid gate closed until around nine o'clock the next morning. The attester was also informed that directly after the death of the *Heer* Alrix the aforementioned d'-Hinoyossa seized all his furniture and furnishings and other moveable and immoveable goods, and took possesion of it, disposing of it as he saw fit. He also knows that at the same time a [   ] disaffection arose between the aforementioned d'Hinoyossa and the *schepenen* of the aforesaid place, whereupon [   ] *schepenen* since then have not filled or exercised their *schepen's* office; and also, that Hinoyossa had the *voorlezer*, Mr. Evert Pietersz fetched from his house to the fort by the *schout* and soldiers.

That he, attester, was informed by his other fellow soldiers and other persons that a chest with magazine's goods was taken out of the house of Gerrit van Sweeringhen, *schout* of the aforesaid place, and brought into the fort, which goods aforesaid Van Sweeringhe had taken from the magazine before the death of the aforementioned *Heer* Alricx.

That he, attester, and other soldiers had received shoes from Gerrit van Sweeringhe from the magazine on their accounts, which shoes they not being pleased with because of the poor quality they often gave sometimes one, sometimes two deer skins for each pair of shoes, receiving then a pair of better shoes, which Van Sweeringhen said were from his own private stock of shoes. The aforesaid Van Sweeringhen then ordered them to keep it quiet and not to let it be known.

That he, attester, also had heard from various people at the aforesaid place that the *Heer* Allexander d'Hinoyossa, after a considerable time had passed since the previous event, when the petitioner was not at home, had the court messenger inform the petitioner's wife that she was to open her chests in order to see what was in there, or otherwise she was to post security for the sum of a thousand guilders. Likewise, he, attester, was also reliably informed that the aforesaid messenger and clerk stayed overnight at the petitioner's house (the petitioner's wife being elsewhere), followed immediately [by the announcement accompanied] by cymbals striking that no one was to attempt to hide the petitioner's wife or any of their goods upon arbitrary punishment. Whereupon Hinoyossa immediately ordered a house search for the petitioner's wife, and all roads and passage ways guarded by soldiers for the purpose of apprehending the petitioner's wife; also, that when the petitioner's child, about four months' old, was apprehended, he, Allexander d'Hinoyossa [   ] to keep it at the house of and with Maria Karremans (being a nursing mother), to which the mother [   ] someone else, being unable to do it, and that the child would be better kept [   ], and that it was given to the messenger's wife for safekeeping. He also declared to know for sure that the aforementioned Allexander de Hinoyossa seized and impounded all the petitioner's possessions at that place for himself, both moveable and immoveable, ordering his clerk and a young [   ] to sleep in the petitioner's house. The attester was also reliably informed that the petitioner, desiring to depart for the Mannates with a galiot skippered by Jacob Jansz Huys in 1661, was detained by d'Hinnoyossa, who forbade the skipper from taking the petitioner along, whereby the petitioner was forced to travel surreptiously overland, because the word had circulated that d'Hinnoyossa was going to put the petitioner in jail. Furthermore, the attester declares that he was also reliably informed that Gerrit van Sweeringhe, from the time that he [   ] the magazine at the place, compensated his servants and carpenters, who built his house and horse mill and helped him during their term of service, always from the aforesaid magazine, and that also during his term he always traded and negotiated in the magazine. All of which precedes or appears in substance, he, the attester, hereby declares to be true and truthful with the offer to confirm the same by solemn oath if required thereto, submitting as basis for knowledge that he, the attester, was continually in the colony's service from the beginning of the colony until the year 1662, and has been present near and in the proximity of the aforesaid. Thus done in Amsteldam, in the presence of Hendrik Bouwmeester and Jacobus Snel as signed etc., this 24th of February 1663.

Henderick van Beyl   Quod attestor
Hendrik Rounsten   Corn. De Grijp Not.
                                 16 2/24 63

[DECLARATION OF GERRIT KOK CONCERNING
ALEXANDER D'HINOYOSSA]

Appeared before me, Cornelis van Poelenburgh, public notary etc., the honorable Gerrit Kok, about 43 years old, residing in this city, who at the request of Cornelis van Gesel has declared and attested that it is true that he, attester, was commissary and councilor at the city's colony of New Amstel on the South River in New Netherland in the year 1664, when a certain Alexander d'Hinoyossa, who served as director, having succeeded to the position of Jacob Alricx, and that he, attester, had heard at that time from reliable persons, officials, burghers, and inhabitants, as well as having seen authentic instruments, accounts, letters and documents, from which he understood and concluded that the aforesaid d'Hinoyossa in the year 165[ ] departed for the aforementioned colony as lieutenant with the aforesaid Alricx as director and commissary general on behalf of this city, and resided there in the aforesaid capacity; but that d'Hinoyossa frequently practiced by improper means to enrich himself with other people's goods; to incite disputes and squabbles among officials, burghers and inhabitants in and outside the colony; to inform poorly and incorrectly the superiors of the colony, to the detriment of those who had been appointed to offices and positions superior and equal to his. Further, he declares that he frequently understood when he heard the inhabitants of the aforesaid colony talking about the aforementioned Jacob Alricx, and also saw from the abovementioned documents that when Alricx passed away in the year 1659, the aforesaid Hinoyossa seized and took possession of his, Alricx's, goods [   ] in spite of the petitioner, both those which the aforesaid Alricx [   ] were under his direction and others [   ] belonged, of which he took possession under pretext of false [   ] according to the disposition of the petitioner and others [   ] and therefore placed himself in possession without making an inventory of them or being willing to inform the petitioner and other heirs about the aforementioned estate or being willing to provide an inventory, denying the petitioner his rights, so that the petitioner was compelled to oppose it [   ]; by which action great reproach was uttered by the fellow officials and other burghers and inhabitants on behalf of d'Hinoyossa. Furthermore, he also heard that the aforementioned d'Hinyossa pursued the petitioner and other heirs because they opposed him, but especially the petitioner, whom he wanted to murder; therefore, it was necessary to attempt to escape. The aforesaid d'Hinyossa not only took hold of the petitioner's wife and child but even impounded their possessions and took from them all they had so that his wife had not even a cloth to clean the baby; and his wife was also able to save herself by fleeing, leaving her baby behind, which they were able to steal from Hinyossa half dead.

Finally, he declares that he lived in the petitioner's house in the year 1664, and that it was used by d'Hinyossa for storing the colony's [   ] and merchandise, which was in his, the attester's, care; also that before he came to live in the petitioner's house, the aforesaid [   ] received the annual rent payments as if it were his own possession. [   ] the aforesaid Hinyossa in the year 1672, being in his majesty's army at Bodegrave, was convicted of inciting to mutiny and executed by the sword subsequent to the sentence pronounced by the honorable and noble [   ]. Of which the attester is ready to the truth, and furthermore confirm by oath. Thus issued in Amsterdam this 25th of May 1675 in the presence of Cornelis Hoogland and Sarvosius Arckentel as witnesses.

Gerardt Kok
Seruos Aertel
Cornelis Hooghlant

> *Quod attestor*
> Cor. van Poelenburgh
> Not. Pub.
> 1675 5/25

Bibliography

Bachman, Van Cleaf. *Peltries or Plantations: The Economic Policies of the Dutch West India Company in New Netherland, 1623–1639*. Baltimore: The Johns Hopkins Press, 1969.

Decker, C.W., editor. *Simon van Leeuwen's Commentaries on Roman–Dutch Law*, translated by Sir John G. Kotze. 2 vols. London: Sweet and Maxwell, Ltd., 1921.

Edwards, Charles S. *Hugo Grotius, The Miracle of Holland: A Study in Political and Legal Thought*. Chicago: Nelson–Hall, 1981.

Fernow, Berthold, editor. *Records of the City of New Amsterdam from 1653 to 1674*. 7 vols. New York: The Knickerbocker Press, 1897. Reprint. Baltimore: Genealogical Publishing Company, 1976.

Fox, Dixon Ryan, editor. *Minutes of the Court of Sessions (1657–1696), Westchester County*. White Plains , N.Y. 1924.

Gehring, Charles T., translator and editor. *New Netherland Documents, Fort Orange Court Minutes, 1652–1660*. Syracuse: Syracuse University Press, 1990.

———. *New York Historical Manuscripts, Council Minutes, 1652–1654*. Baltimore: Genealogical Publishing Company, 1983.

———. *New York Historical Manuscripts, Delaware Papers: Dutch Period*. Baltimore: Genealogical Publishing Company, 1981.

———. *New York Historical Manuscripts, Land Papers, 1630–1664*. Baltimore: Genealogical Publishing Company, 1980.

Geyl, P. *The Revolt of the Netherlands (1555–1609)*. London: Williams & Norgate Ltd., 1932.

Jameson, J. Franklin, editor. *Narratives of New Netherland, 1609–1664*. New York: C. Scribner's Sons, 1909. Reprint. New York: Barnes and Noble, 1967.

151

O'Callaghan, E. B., editor. *Calendar of Historical Manuscripts*. 2 vols. Albany: Weed, Parsons and Co., 1864–1865. Reprint. Ridgewood, N.J.: Gregg Press, 1968.

————, translator and editor. *Documents Relative to the Colonial History of the State of New York.* 15 vols. Albany: Weed, Parsons and Company, 1856–1887. Vols. 12–15 translated and edited by Berthold Fernow.

————, translator and editor. *Laws and Ordinances of New Netherland, 1638–1674.* Albany: Weed, Parsons and Co., 1868.

Parker, Geoffery. *The Dutch Revolt*. Ithaca: Cornell University Press, 1977.

Rink, Oliver A. *Holland on the Hudson: An Economic and Social History of Dutch New York*. Ithaca: Cornell University Press, 1986.

Stokes, I. N. P. *Iconography of Manhattan Island, 1498–1909*. 6 vols. New York: R. H. Dodd, 1915–28. Reprint. New York: Arno Press, 1967.

Van Laer, A.J.F., translator and editor. *Documents Relating To New Netherland, 1624–1626, in The Henry E. Huntington Library*. San Marino: The Henry E. Huntington Library and Art Gallery, 1924.

————. *Minutes of the Court of Rensselaerswyck, 1648–1652*. Albany: University of the State of New York, 1922.

————. *New York Historical Manuscripts, Council Minutes, 1638–1649*. Edited by Kenneth Scott and Kenn Stryker-Rodda. Baltimore: Genealogical Publishing Company, 1974.

————. *New York Historical Manuscripts, Registers of the Provincial Secretary (1638–1660)*. Edited by Kenneth Scott and Kenn Stryker-Rodda. 3 vols. Baltimore: Genealogical Publishing Company, 1974.

————. *Van Rensselaer Bowier Manuscripts*. Albany: University of the State of New York, 1908.

Versteeg, Dingman, translator. *New York Historical Manuscripts, Kingston Papers, 1661–1675*. Edited by Peter R. Christoph, Kenneth Scott, and Kenn Stryker-Rodda. 2 vols. Baltimore: Genealogical Publishing Company, 1976.

Wessels, J.W. *History of the Roman–Dutch Law*. Grahamstown, Cape Colony: African Book Company, 1908.

Index

Abrahams, Marritgen, to administer husband's estate 131–32

Aertel/Arckentel, Seruos/Sarvosius, witness to deposition 149

Africa, mentioned xiv

agriculture, injured by bakers 26; promotion of 32, 98–100

Ahasimus/Jersey City, New Jersey, mentioned 63n, 85n

Albany, see Beverwijck

Albertsz, Albert, arbitrator 122–23

alcohol (beer, brandy, liquor, spirits, wine), brewing and sale restricted 4, 22; ferry fees 42; forfeit 22; on holidays 53; permit for 16; permitted without excise 27; price of 25–27, 34, 36, 52, 88; on Sabbath 3, 8, 16, 71–72, 83–84; sale to Indians 3, 9, 14–15, 18, 47–48, 83–84; smuggled 6, 21; taxes on 12, 33–34, 37–38, 54, 60–61, 78–79, 109; unloading fee 65; mentioned 24

Allerton, Isaac, mortgage on le Feber farm 112

Alrichs/Alricx, Jacob, New Amstel director and commissary general, death of 139–46; estate of 120–22, inventoried 137–39, seized 148, settled 115–16

Alrichs/Alrix, Pieter, heir of J. Alrichs 115–16, 137

Amesfoort Flat/Great Flat/Bay, court formed at xvii; land title of Gerritsen and Hudde annulled 30

Amsterdam/Amsteldam, Holland, burgher right 80; burgomasters of, mentioned 145; creditors in 134–35; deposition taken in 145, 148–49; edicts and ordinances, mentioned xix; estate inventoried in 137; exclusion of Jews from militia 50; burgomasters, ad-

minister New Amstel 115n; slaughter excise 53n; statutes about brawling 5; weights and measures 5, 57; mentioned xvi, xviii, xix, 35n

Amsterdam, New Netherland, see New Amsterdam

anchorage, see shipping

Anglo-Dutch War, first, mentioned 39n; third, mentioned xvi

Anthony, Allard, suits with De Moore 110–11, Huys 105–6, van Couwenhoven 109

appraising and assessing, ordinance 92–94

arbitrators, court of, formed xvii

Arckentel, Sarvosius, see Aertel, Seruos

Arminius, Jacobus, theologian, mentioned xiii

arms, excise used for 54; guns fired in New Amsterdam 32, not to be fired at night 40–41; knives and swords, fighting with 5, 8, 45; munitions, expensive 46; powder wasted 52; sale banned of carbines, munitions, parts of guns 62–63; soldiers to have powder and lead 68–69, side arms 45, weapons 67–69; mentioned 100

Artcher, John, alias Jan Coopall, suit with Panton 107–8, 111–12

Atkins, Hatton, suit with Culpeper 133

attorney, vander Veen for Schut 112

Baker, Jacob, arbitrator 113n

Baltic wars, mentioned xv

Barnegat Bay, mentioned xv

barrels or casks, tobacco to be packed in 49

Barsimson, Jacob, suit with Wessels 109–10

LAWS & WRITS OF APPEAL

was composed in Times Roman on a Northgate 386/20
by New Netherland Project;
printed by sheet-fed offset on 60-pound, acid-free Glatfelter Natural Hi Bulk
and Smyth-sewn and bound over binder's boards in Holliston Roxite B
by Braun–Brumfield, Inc.;
and published by

SYRACUSE UNIVERSITY PRESS
SYRACUSE, NEW YORK 13244–5160